Editor
Janet Cain

Editorial Project Manager
Elizabeth Morris, Ph.D.

Editor in Chief
Sharon Coan, M.S. Ed.

Illustrators
Sue Fullam
Blanca Apodaca

Cover Artist
Jose Tapia

Art Coordinator
Denice Adorno

Art Director
Richard D'sa

Imaging
James Edward Grace

Product Manager
Phil Garcia

Acknowledgements
Netscape Communicator
screenshots © 2000 Netscape
Communications Corporation.
America Online screenshots ©
2000 America Online, Inc. Used
with permission. Netscape,
Netscape Navigator, Netscape
Communicator, and the N logo
are trademarks of Netscape
Communications Corporation in
the United States and other
countries. America Online,
AOL, and the AOL logo are
registered trademarks of
America Online, Inc. in the
United States and other
countries.

Publishers
Rachelle Cracchiolo, M.S. Ed.
Mary Dupuy Smith, M.S. Ed.

Early Childhood Activities

with

Internet Connections

Author

Grace Jasmine

Teacher Created Materials, Inc.
6421 Industry Way
Westminster, CA 92683
www.teachercreated.com

ISBN-1-57690-468-7

©2000 Teacher Created Materials, Inc.
Made in U.S.A.

Teacher Created Materials

Table of Contents

Introduction

The Internet Is Everywhere

Many people are interested in what the Internet has to offer. Everywhere you look you find another article about the "information highway" and the various ways this tool can prove useful to you—for doing research, reading books online, ordering airline tickets, conducting personal banking, shopping, and much more.

Many teachers actively use the Internet to enhance their curriculum, even at the early childhood level. It is likely that children you teach today will someday use computers and the Internet as part of their daily lives, both in the work place and at home.

With this in mind, children are being given opportunities to use computers starting at an increasingly early age. It makes sense for early childhood educators to use the computer as part of their regular classroom routine. To meet this demand, companies that specialize in creating children's software have expanded their product lines to include programs specifically for babies and toddlers.

Technology and Young Children

The National Association for the Education of Young Children (NAEYC) has been paying careful attention to the impact that computer technology is having on the world. They are concerned with how technology is being used to prepare young children for a future in the information age. In the April 1996 Position Statement on Technology and Young Children, NAEYC states:

> Technology plays a significant role in all aspects of American life today, and this role will only increase in the future. The potential benefits of technology for young children's learning and development are well documented. As technology becomes easier to use . . . young children's use of technology becomes more widespread. Therefore, early childhood educators have a responsibility to critically examine the impact of technology on children and be prepared to use technology to benefit children. (NAEYC, 1996)

Note: You may download a copy of NAEYC's Position Statement on Technology and Young Children by visiting the following Web site:

http://www.naeyc.org/about/position/pstech98.htm

Introduction *(cont.)*

The Internet as a Classroom Tool

The only reason to use any tool in your classroom or educational facility is to benefit children. This book is designed with that purpose in mind—to help you easily and effectively use various aspects of the Internet to enrich the learning experiences of children you teach.

NAEYC states that the use of technology in the classroom should be "*. . . integrated into the regular learning environment and used as one of the many options to support children's learning.*" (1996)

This book will help you combine your lessons and centers into thematic units that include use of the Internet. The Internet is a tool to facilitate your plans, ideas, and early childhood curriculum. Since the Internet is the largest and most complete audio-visual reference library in the world, there are an infinite number of sites that you can use to illustrate and emphasize every area of instruction.

An Integrated, Thematic Approach

In this book, the Internet and World Wide Web are intended to be used as a springboard that will help you provide interesting up-to-date and media-rich information about a variety of subjects that you and your children will enjoy exploring.

The Internet is just like a library in that it is more important that you know where to look for information than to be able to identify a specific source. *Early Childhood Activities with Internet Connections* builds activities around using the Internet as a reference tool. To prepare for the hands-on computer activities described in this book, it is suggested that you locate, bookmark, and save the Web sites ahead of time. This way you will not have to spend valuable instructional time searching for appropriate sites.

A Teacher Resource

The Internet is a wonderful reference tool for early childhood professionals. You can network, contact early childhood organizations, talk to other educators, and/or become part of one or more mailing lists. You can plan lessons, do research, take classes, and enhance your ability to be the kind of teacher who makes an ever-increasing positive impact on the lives of children you teach.

Organization of the Book

Early Childhood Activities with Internet Connections is organized into four parts to focus on the areas of science, social studies, mathematics, and language and the arts. Each part is divided into four thematic units. Each unit includes Annotated Web Sites to help you get started with Internet research, hands-on Internet experiences to use with children, a take-home storybook for children to share with their families, and a wide variety of cross-curricular activities.

For example, the unit on oceans includes a(an):

- Internet Web site about oceans
- Internet Web site about whales
- science discovery lesson about pet fish
- art experience to make an ocean mobile
- hands-on cooking exercise to make ocean cookies
- take-home storybook about betta fish

Features of the Book

Early Childhood Activities with Internet Connections features some of these fascinating experiences for children. You and your students will be able to do the following:

- Watch and listen to a professional tap dancer
- Send questions to a reptile expert and get answers
- View the Earth as if you were standing on the moon
- Listen to hundreds of children's songs
- See places and children from around the world
- Communicate with other children who also have Internet connections
- Make digital photographs
- Take a close-up look at bugs, without getting dirty
- Publish pictures, stories, and other work
- Record your voices
- Create a classroom art gallery
- Tour the White House
- Write a letter to the President
- Make friends around the world using e-mail
- Play games, color pictures, and learn skills
- Use e-mail to send pictures and voice recordings to parents and/or friends

Purpose of the Book

This book is intended for use by early childhood educators who are interested in the following:

- Using the Internet as part of their early childhood curriculum
- Integrating the computer and the Internet as instructional tools
- Taking advantage of the many opportunities and learning experiences the Internet has to offer early childhood students
- Teaching thematic units that have Internet connections
- Helping children become computer literate
- Using cross-curricular activities

Adapting the Book to Suit Your Needs

This book makes it easy for you to integrate computers and the Internet into your existing centers and curriculum in a meaningful and interesting way. Each unit includes the information and instructions for all of the lessons. While the units are designed as weekly plans, you may wish to adapt them depending on the needs of your students and your teaching style.

Here are a few suggestions for ways to adapt this book.

- Use the Internet on a daily basis with your students, or have children go online only on days when you have classroom helpers.
- Have children use the Internet as a whole class, in small groups, with partners, or on an individual basis.
- Use the Internet to prepare and present lessons, or allow time for students to do hands-on Internet activities.

As you use the lessons in this book, you will discover what works best for you and your students.

How to Plan and Use a Unit

Annotated Web Sites

This is a short list of annotated Web sites to help you get started doing research on a particular subject. You may find it helpful to bookmark these sites for future reference. Use any of these four annotated sites—along with others mentioned in the Technology Take-Off Points at the end of each thematic activity. In addition, a list of suggested keywords are provided that will help you search for additional information related to the annotated sites. Be sure to bookmark your favorite sites as you explore, so that you can return to them again and again.

Hands-On Computer Activities

These hands-on activities introduce children to the Internet. To reduce the time you may have to spend waiting for a specific Web site, most activities suggest types of sites rather than specific sites. All activities are structured so you can preview the sites before using them with children.

Thematic Activities

A unit may begin with an Internet activity and then move to a thematic exploration. Children learn that the Internet is a tool they can use as part of their learning experiences.

Storybook

A unit's theme is introduced using a take-home storybook, providing a wonderful opportunity to promote early literacy and teach reading readiness skills. These take-home storybooks can also connect school and home, involving families in learning experiences.

Technology Teaching Tip

These are fun, do-it-yourself computer activities designed for early childhood educators to learn what is available on the Internet without being technology experts.

Technology for Children

These learn-by-doing activities help introduce children to computer basics. Each of these activities teaches a particular computer skill that children will need now and in the future. The activities appear in every other unit and include instructions for PC and Macintosh (MAC).

Breakdown of Activities

Each activity is divided into some or all of the following easy-to-use parts:

- Approximate Preparation Time
- Materials
- Directed Teaching Focus
- At the Computer
- Technology Take-Off Point
- Learning Concept
- Lesson Preparation
- Self-Directed Activity
- What to Say

Suggested Two-Week Schedule

You can use any of the activities in this book in any way that best suits the needs of your students. The following suggested schedule is intended to give you a sense of how a unit might be organized.

Week One

Monday	Preview the unit. Read the activities and gather supplies needed for the unit.
Tuesday	Preview the sites suggested in the Annotated Web Sites and bookmark those that interest you. Use these sites as a springboard for your own online exploration. Use the Suggested Keyword Searches to look for additional sites. Make sure to bookmark sites that you like, so you can hold on to your favorites. Decide if you will use parent helpers for any Internet or thematic activities in the unit and schedule them for next week.
Wednesday	Go through the Technology Teaching Tip, which is an activity designed for you. This portion of the book provides you with some easy Internet options that will help you learn a lot without getting too technical.
Thursday	See the storybook ideas on page 9 to plan for each story presentation. Use the directions on page 10 for making a big book version of each storybook.
Friday	Introduce the unit using the big book version storybook during Circle Time. Give children their own copies of the storybook to color and take home. Explain to children that on Monday they will be learning more about the subject of the unit, and give them some examples of the activities to come.

Week Two

Prepare anything that you need for the unit. Determine when you are going to present each activity. Remember that the presentation of the unit does not have to be done in one or two weeks. You might want to take longer depending on children's interest level and any other related activities that you would like to use.

Monday	Technology activity (if applicable) Hands-on Internet activity
Tuesday	Thematic activity Review of storybook, using an additional storybook idea from page 9.
Wednesday	Hands-on Internet activity
Thursday	Thematic activity
Friday	Final thematic activity Internet activities review Personal review (Spend a few minutes deciding which activities were your favorites and what you might do differently next time.)

Special Whole-Book Themes

There are some exciting extras in this book that make it special. Look for the following whole-book themes:

Take-Home Stories

As an early childhood educator, you know that it is important to you and often a challenge to bring the rich and rewarding world of books into the lives of children you teach.

Since some children do not have any books at home and come to school without having been exposed to reading, each unit in *Early Childhood Activities with Internet Connections* features a black line master for a take-home storybook that relates to the theme.

These storybooks:

- provide instant home libraries or allow children to expand existing home libraries.
- are an excellent home-school connection that will help support children's learning.
- serve to emphasize the importance of literacy and reading readiness skills for young children.
- provide opportunities for youngsters to read and reread age-appropriate stories.

Class Cooking Experience and Cookbook

Many of the units in this book feature a cooking experience. After you have used the cooking lessons in this book, reproduce the cookbook cover (page 13) and the recipes. Allow children to take their cookbooks home to share with their families. Encourage parents to try the recipes at home. Tell parents to keep the cookbook as a reminder of the fun their children had in your class.

Technology Teaching Tips

The addendum at the end of the book has technology teaching tips. It contains a hands-on Internet or computer experience designed just for teachers. Think of this section of the book as a book within a book—an early childhood educator's guide to using many facets of the Internet.

Mini-lessons include:
- selecting an Internet Service Provider (ISP)
- sending and receiving e-mail

All you have to do to use these activities is set aside some time and work through the step-by-step directions. This book highlights some of the Internet products and services that you may find useful without being overly technical. Anyone, regardless of the amount of experience you already have, can learn to use the tools described.

Making Storybooks

For each unit, make a big book version of the storybook. Read the big book during Circle Time to introduce the unit.

Materials for the Big Book Storybooks

- poster board, one piece for every two pages of the storybook
- enlarged storybook masters
- glue
- markers (various colors)

Directions

1. Enlarge the story master to 11" x 14" (28 cm x 36 cm), and color it.
2. Glue the enlarged story master pages to poster board.
3. Laminate the big book.
4. Punch three holes along the left-hand side of each piece of poster board, and insert individual binder rings.

Materials for Student Storybooks

- storybook masters (one set for each unit)
- We Read master (page 11)
- Parent Letter (page 12)

Read the Story

Introduce the story at Circle Time using the big book storybook. Provide children with stapled copies of the storybook. Invite them to take their books home to share with their families. This way you can introduce the story and remind parents of your "We Read" home and school reading readiness storybook concept.

Suggested Storybook Extensions

Following is a list of suggested storybook extensions for the units in Part One. Use these and any others that you would like. Use similar types of extensions for the other units in this book.

Unit	Storybook Title	Extensions
One	Beautiful Betta Fish	• Purchase some fish and have children observe them. • Have children draw fish. • Go back online to check out betta sites.
Two	The Planets	• Have children draw planets on the pavement using chalk.
Three	Little Flower's Happy Day	• Invite children to use creative dramatics to act out the part of the flower and the weather elements in the story. • Walk around the school grounds to look for signs of growth in plants.
Four	A Visit to the Zoo	• Take children on a field trip to a real zoo. • Invite guest speakers to bring interesting animals to class for children to see.

We Read!

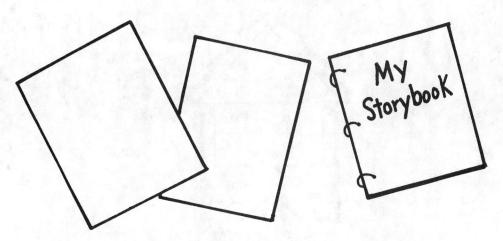

Take-Home Storybooks

for

Children and Their Families

Storybook Title:_____

This storybook belongs to _____.

Teacher: _____ Date: _____

Parent Letter

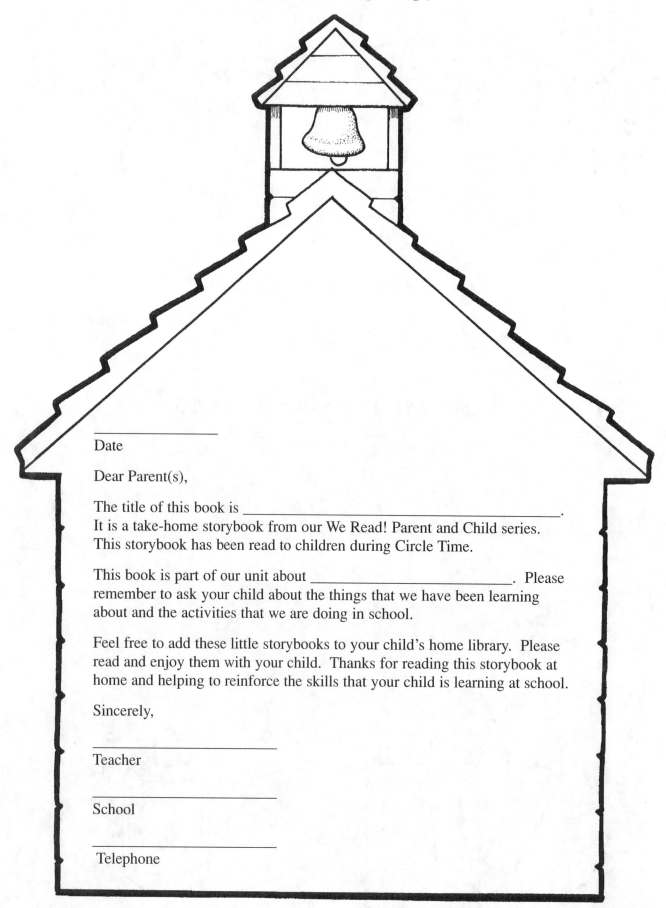

_____
Date

Dear Parent(s),

The title of this book is _____.
It is a take-home storybook from our We Read! Parent and Child series.
This storybook has been read to children during Circle Time.

This book is part of our unit about _____. Please
remember to ask your child about the things that we have been learning
about and the activities that we are doing in school.

Feel free to add these little storybooks to your child's home library. Please
read and enjoy them with your child. Thanks for reading this storybook at
home and helping to reinforce the skills that your child is learning at school.

Sincerely,

_____
Teacher

_____
School

_____
Telephone

We Cook!

Class Cookbook

This cookbook belongs to _____.

Teacher's Name: _____

School Year: _____

Internet Basics

Internet Center Requirements

For an Internet Center, you must have the following:

- computer, including a color monitor (screen), mouse, and keyboard
- internal or external modem
- classroom phone line to which you can connect the modem
- computer printer, preferably one that prints in color
- surge protector
- account with an Internet Service Provider (ISP)
- operating system
- Internet browser
- antivirus software (see below)
- safety software (page 15)

Setting Up Your Internet Center

Keep in mind the following points when setting up your Internet center:

- Remember to give yourself a comfortable place to sit while you are researching and previewing Web sites, sending and receiving e-mail, and manipulating the mouse during classroom demonstrations.

- Seats for children should allow them to have a clear view of the screen during demonstrations. If children need to have access to the mouse and keyboard, be sure their seats are at an appropriate height to reach the equipment.

- Make the Internet Center a water- and food-free zone.

- Remind children to wash their hands before touching the computer equipment. Stress that they should never touch the screen so that everyone can enjoy a clear, clean view of the pictures and information on the computer.

- Keep the Central Processing Unit (CPU), which is the "brain" of your computer, in a safe, clean location. Keep in mind that many of today's tower-type units can be easily tipped and could fall on a child.

- For safety reasons, keep cords and wires shortened with twist ties or rubber bands, and keep them from crossing traffic areas.

- Don't overload electrical outlets. Use a power strip with a surge protection device. The extra cost for this piece of equipment is small, but the benefits are very big.

- Use antivirus software. MacAfee, Norton, and other companies offer comprehensive antivirus utilities at affordable prices. Both MacAfee and Norton operate Web sites that allow registered users to upgrade their software in order to detect and combat current viruses.

- Don't be afraid to ask for help. Sources for helpful information include computer stores, phone numbers for help desks found in hardware and software manuals, computer books, or Web sites on the Internet.

Safeguards and Permissions

Protecting Yourself and Your Students

The Internet is the product of international free speech. As a result, some Web sites are NOT appropriate for children. It is your responsibility to protect children in your classroom from accessing these sites. Remember the five basic safety rules listed below when using the Internet with your students.

- ALWAYS monitor children who are using the Internet.
- ALWAYS be sure to preview any Web sites that you plan to visit with your students.
- NEVER post or publish any personal information.
- NEVER publish a child's photo, voice, or work without parental consent.
- NEVER let a child participate in Internet activities without a signed parental consent form. Be sure to provide other theme-related activities for students who are not allowed to do the Internet lessons.

Parent Permission

Inform your building administrator about using the Internet with your students. Make sure you adhere to your district, campus, or facility Internet use policies. Before a child is allowed to use the Internet, be sure you get a signed parental consent form. Check to see if there is an official consent form that must be used. If no form is available, you may wish to use the one provided on page 16. In addition, a Web site that contains a sampling of Acceptable Use Policies in English and Spanish follows:

http://chico.rice.edu/armadillo/Rice/Resources/acceptable.html

Information and Demonstrations

To reinforce parents' confidence in your safety precautions, you may wish to schedule Internet demonstrations for parents. Show parents what children are experiencing in your classroom and how family members can extend that learning at home.

Volunteers in Your Classroom

Make sure that everyone who volunteers to help with Internet activities in your classroom knows and agrees to abide by your Internet safety rules. Possible helpers include older students, parents, senior citizens, and community volunteers.

Software for Safety

There are several Internet blocking packages available that will attempt to keep your browser from connecting to inappropriate Web sites. However, the only way to guarantee that children will not access an inappropriate site is to be sure you always preview sites that your students will see.

Internet Safety Plan

Take the time and precaution of writing down and posting your Internet safety plan. The parental permission letter on page 16 has the basic elements that a plan should include.

Parent Permission for Internet Activities

_____
Date

Dear Parent,

This year we will be using our classroom computer to connect to the information resource called the Internet. I have posted a copy of my Internet safety plan near the computer. Volunteers who help children with computer lessons must agree to abide by this safety plan. Major elements of the plan include the following:

- Children will only be able to get to Web sites that have been previewed and approved by me.
- Children will use the Internet only with permission and adult supervision.
- Your child's personal information—such as name, address, and phone number—will NEVER be used on the Internet.

Our class is very excited about integrating this technology to our existing curriculum. I look forward to having parents be an active part of these learning experiences. I encourage you to come observe our class and/or to become an Internet activity volunteer. Please call me if you have any questions or concerns or if you would like to observe or volunteer.

Sincerely,

_____
Teacher

_____
School

_____
Phone

- -

PERMISSION SLIP

Child's Name: _____

Please check all that apply. Then sign and return the form to me by _____.

❑ YES, my child MAY participate in classroom Internet activities with adult supervision.

❑ YES, my child MAY use e-mail with adult supervision.

❑ YES, my child's photograph, voice, and work MAY be used in e-mail or e-mail attachments.

❑ NO, my child MAY NOT participate in Internet activities in the classroom.

❑ NO, my child MAY NOT use e-mail.

Parent's Signature: _____ Date: _____

Parent's Printed Name: _____

Oceans

Hands-On Internet Activities

Whale Watching

The Ocean

Thematic Activities

Science—Classroom Pet Fish and Fishy Science

Art—Gifts from the Sea Mobile

Cooking—Ocean Cookies

Storybook—Beautiful Betta Fish

Annotated Web Sites

Shell World's Cyber Island

http://www.seashellworld.com/seashells.htm

This site offers a wonderful array of seashell photographs. It also sells shells.

Whales on the Net

http://whales.magna.com.au/home.html

This site has information, photographs, and links for all kinds of whales. There is an interesting FAQ (frequently asked questions) section, and you can e-mail the Webmaster with questions about whales. This site requires a long time to load.

Virtual Whales

http://www.cs.sfu.ca/research/projects/Whales/

This multimedia site offers sound clips and movies of whales. It takes a long time to load.

WhaleNet Slide Show

http://whale.wheelock.edu/whalenet-stuff/slide_shows/

This site has a multitude of whale pictures.

The Evergreen Project's Temperate Oceans

http://www.mobot.org/mbgnet/salt/oceans/index.htm

This site has basic information about oceans and includes beautiful pictures produced by the Evergreen Project, an educational company in St. Louis.

Gray Whales with Winston

http://www.geocities.com/RainForest/Jungle/1953/index.html

Learn about the gray whale with Winston, an animated dog. This enjoyable, easy-to-understand site has lots of pictures of whales.

Suggested Keyword Searches

shells, seashells, whales, ocean, ocean life, sea life, sea animals, fish, bettas, betta fish (You may also wish to search for specific types of whales, such as killer whales and gray whales.)

Whale Watching

Approximate Preparation Time

30 minutes

Learning Concept

Children will be able to recognize and name the various parts of the whale as well as distinguish at least two different types of whales. This activity enhances children's vocabulary and oral language skills, as well as a knowledge and understanding of basic biology.

Materials

- classroom computer
- Internet Service Provider (ISP)
- bookmarked Web sites (page 17)
- Parts of a Whale (page 19), one for each child; one enlarged copy

- white construction paper, one piece for each child
- crayons or markers
- printer
- printer paper

Lesson Preparation

Preview and bookmark whale sites that you intend to use with students. Reproduce the Parts of a Whale black line master, making one for each student and an enlarged copy for your lesson introduction.

Circle Time

Use the enlarged version of the Parts of a Whale black line master to introduce this lesson. As you name parts of the whale, have children point to these parts on their black line copies. Prepare children for the Internet experience by telling them that they will use the Internet to see photographs of real whales. Mention the things that you want children to notice about the whales, such as color, shape, size, unique features, and behavior. Encourage children to take home their copies of the Parts of a Whale.

At the Computer

Allow children to view pictures of the whales. Ask them to vote to pick their favorite whale picture. Then print that picture. As an alternative, have each child pick a whale to draw. Display the printed picture or drawn pictures on a bulletin board. Discuss why children picked the whale(s) they did.

What to Say

Today we are going to go whale watching, but we don't need to be on a boat in the ocean. We can do it in our very own classroom. Let's all sit around the computer, and I will show you some great pictures of real whales. We will vote to choose the whale picture we like best. Then we will print the picture and hang it on the bulletin board in our classroom. (You may prefer to have children draw and color pictures of whales to display.)

Parts of a Whale

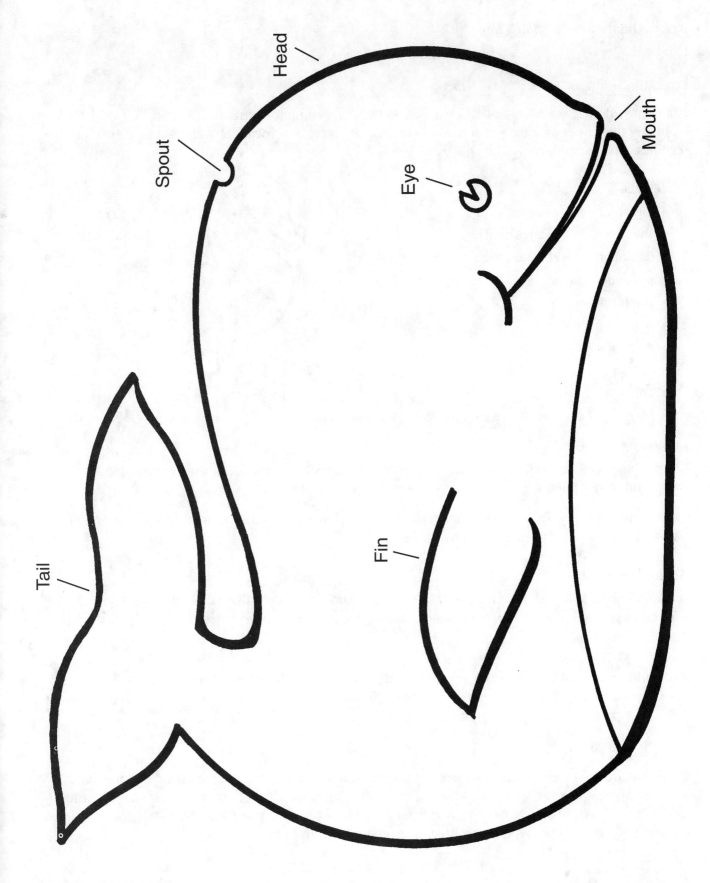

The Ocean

Approximate Preparation Time

two hours

Learning Concept

Children will increase their knowledge of sea animals and begin to learn related scientific vocabulary, including the names of some sea animals. This activity increases vocabulary and improves reading readiness and memorization skills.

Materials

- classroom computer
- Internet Service Provider (ISP)
- bookmarked Web sites (page 17)
- computer printer
- printer paper
- butcher paper
- tape or staples
- scissors
- construction paper
- blue water color or poster paint or blue construction paper

Lesson Preparation

Preview and bookmark whale sites that you intend to use with students. Choose sites that have wonderful sea pictures.

Prepare the mural by drawing an oceanscape using poster paints or watercolors or by cutting and gluing blue construction paper onto the butcher paper.

At the Computer

Ask children to join you at the computer to see the pictures of sea life that you have bookmarked. Talk with children about the sea life you examine and have each choose a favorite.

Center Time

Ask children to draw their favorite type of sea life. You may wish to have them cut out their pictures. Then have children pick a place in the mural that they would like to place their pictures. Help them staple or tape the pictures onto the mural.

What to Say

Today we are going to use our computer to visit the ocean. We will be looking at some of the plants and animals that live in the ocean. After we look at the pictures, each of you will pick your favorite kind of sea life. It is okay if more than one person picks a certain type of sea life. Then you will draw a picture of your favorite type of sea life to put on our ocean mural.

Classroom Pet Fish

Approximate Preparation Time

one hour

Learning Concept

Children help set up a habitat for a live fish. By doing this, they learn about living things and the responsibilities of pet ownership. In addition, they improve their ability to listen to and follow directions and expand their oral language and reading readiness skills.

Materials

- Beautiful Betta Fish storybook (pages 28–32)
- betta* or goldfish
- fish bowl
- gravel or glass aquarium balls
- fish food
- plastic plant, rock and/or other decorations
- water dechlorination drops (for adult use only)
- art paper
- crayons or markers

*NOTE: Male bettas can live in fish bowls. They are easy to care for, colorful, and inexpensive. These hearty fish thrive in an unfiltered glass bowl with a weekly water change.

Lesson Preparation

Set up an Art Center with paper and crayons or markers. Obtain the materials for the fish bowl. Reproduce the storybook Beautiful Betta Fish.

Directed Teaching Focus

Read and discuss the storybook Beautiful Betta Fish. Talk about how to care for living things such as pets. Read books about fish.

Self-Directed Activity

After the fish is in the bowl, allow children to draw pictures of it. Display the pictures or bind them into a book. You can also write stories that children dictate to you about their pictures.

What to Say

We are going to make a home for a betta fish. (Show children the fish.) You can tell this is a male, or boy, betta because it has longer fins and is more colorful than a female, or girl. To get his bowl ready, we need to fill it with water. I will add some special drops that make the water clean for a fish. I am the only one who may touch these drops. Next we add some colored balls, a plant, and a rock. Then we will put the fish in the bowl. Now let's talk about the betta's food. (Lead a discussion.) Who can think of a name for our fish? (Write the names on the board. Allow the class to vote for their favorite name.)

Technology Take-Off Point

Betta enthusiasts make their own Web sites. Search for "betta" on the Web and you will find a number of interesting sites to share with students.

Fishy Science

Approximate Preparation Time

30 minutes

Learning Concept

Children conduct two simple science experiments using a live fish. This activity enhances cognitive thinking, the ability to understand cause-and-effect relationships, and oral language skills.

Materials

- science observation materials
- construction paper, various colors
- cassette or CD player
- different types of music, such as country, children's, classical, rock, jazz
- art paper
- crayons or markers

Lesson Preparation

Have your classroom fish and fishbowl set up as described on page 21. Prepare for following two experiments.

Experiment One: Does our fish have a favorite color?

Give each child a piece of construction paper. Be sure each child gets a different color. Have children, one at a time, hold the colored paper next to the fishbowl. Ask: *Does the fish look at the paper? Does he swim toward or away from it? Does he act differently with different colors? Does he have a favorite color? How can you tell?*

Experiment Two: Does our fish have a favorite type of music?

Talk about the different kinds of music. Identify each type for children. Play the different types of music for the fish. Ask: *Does the fish swim more during a certain type of music? Does the fish seem to like one kind of music more than another type of music? How can you tell?*

Directed Teaching Focus

Review the storybook Beautiful Betta Fish. End each day by talking about your pet fish and what children notice about his behavior. Have children use the five senses as a springboard for the discussion. Examples: *What do you think the fish can see? What do you think he can hear?*

Self-Directed Activity

Have children draw pictures to show the results of the experiments.

Technology Take-Off Point

Get additional science ideas or subscribe to an inexpensive newsletter from the following site: **http://www.sciencemadesimple.com/**

As an alternative, go to **http://www.ask.com** and search for sites by typing this question: *Where can I find science activities for young children?*

Gifts from the Sea Mobile

Approximate Preparation Time

one hour

Learning Concept

In this art experience, children explore the texture, color, and shape of natural items from the ocean or seashore and they make a mobile. This lesson enhances fine motor coordination and spatial relations.

Materials

- wire coat hanger, one for each child
- yarn, cut to various lengths
- items from the ocean such as shells, sand, and driftwood
- Fish and Shell Patterns (page 24)
- crayons
- scissors
- laminator and laminating film or clear Contact™ paper (optional)
- hole punch
- plastic or paper bowls

Lesson Preparation

Make an Art Center with all of the materials children will need to make their mobiles. You may wish to invite a volunteer to help children at the center. Reproduce the fish and shell patterns. Depending on the level of children you teach, you may want to pre-cut and punch holes in the patterns. Place the shell patterns in one bowl and the fish patterns in another bowl.

Display shells, sand, driftwood, and other ocean items. These can be purchased at most craft stores.

Directed Teaching Focus

Talk with children about gifts from the sea. Examine the shells, sand, driftwood, and other items in the ocean. Talk about how people can protect the ocean environment. Demonstrate how to make the mobile. Provide help to children who need it.

Self-Directed Activity

Allow children to examine the real shells and other items from the ocean. You may wish to have children create their mobiles as a self-directed activity. To improve the durability of the fish and shell patterns, laminate them or cover them with clear Contact™ paper after children color them.

What to Say

(Point out that ocean and sea mean the same thing.) Today we are going to make mobiles with pictures of fish and shells. Pick three fish and three shells for your mobile. Color them any way you like. Then string a piece of yarn though each hole and tie it. Tie the other end of the yarn to the hanger. (As you explain, model how to put the mobile together.)

Technology Take-Off Point

Learn about shells by visiting the following Web site:

http://www.seashellworld.com/seashells.htm

Fish and Shell Patterns

Ocean Cookies

Approximate Preparation Time

30 minutes

Learning Concept

In this lesson, children learn to listen to and follow a sequence of directions, while improving their understanding of measurement concepts and fine motor coordination.

Materials

- ingredients and recipe for Ocean Cookies (page 26) or pre-packaged sugar cookie dough
- ingredients and recipe for Ocean Frosting Recipe (page 26) or canned white frosting with blue food coloring
- Ocean Cookies Sequence Cards (page 27), one copy for each child
- toaster oven
- plastic bowls

- measuring cups and measuring spoons
- electric mixer or hand beaters
- cookie sheets
- spatula
- oven mitts
- rolling pin (optional)
- cookie cutters (optional)
- chewy, fruit-flavored fish candy

Warnings: Ask parents if their children have any food allergies or dietary restrictions. Never allow children near the hot toaster oven or to handle anything that is hot.

Lesson Preparation

Make cookies from scratch (page 26), or use a store-bought sugar cookie dough. Set up a Cooking Center with the recipe and ingredients for making sugar cookies. Arrange children's seating so that the lesson can be presented to the whole class or small groups. You may wish to enlist the help of volunteers.

Remember to reproduce the recipe for the class cookbook and for student cookbooks that will be sent home at the end of the year. Reproduce the sequence cards for children. Cut the cards apart and place each set in a resealable plastic bag. Encourage children to take home the cards.

Directed Teaching Focus

Discuss the order of steps for the recipe. Then help children make the cookies.

Self-Directed Activity

Have children decorate their cookies with blue frosting and chewy, fruit-flavored fish candy.

What to Say

Today we are going to make Ocean Cookies. First we will make the cookies together. Then each of you will decorate your own Ocean Cookie. (Help children make the cookies and icing.)

Technology Take-Off Point

Talk about how to use the Internet to find out more about cookies and recipes. Spend time browsing **http://www.cookierecipe.com/** to see a database of recipes.

Ocean Recipes

Ocean Cookies Recipe

Ingredients

1 cup (250 mL) butter

2 cups (500 mL) sugar

2 eggs

1/2 cup (125 mL) milk

1/2 teaspoon (2.5 mL) vanilla

3 3/4 cups (900 mL) flour

4 teaspoons (20 mL) baking powder

Directions

In a bowl, cream together the butter, sugar, and vanilla. Sift the flour and baking powder into a separate bowl. In another bowl, beat together the eggs and milk. Pour this liquid into the sugar mixture and slowly add the sifted flour and baking power. Shape the dough into a thick roll and chill for two hours. Slice the dough and bake it at 350 degrees for 10 to 15 minutes. Baking times may vary depending on the thickness of the sliced dough.

Alternative

You may also roll this dough and cut it with cookie cutters if you wish.

Ocean Frosting Recipe

Ingredients

1/2 cup (125 mL) butter

2 1/2 cups (625 mL) powdered sugar

1/4 cup (60 mL) milk

1 teaspoon (5 mL) vanilla

blue food coloring

Directions

In a bowl, thoroughly cream together the butter and sugar with an electric mixer or hand beaters. Add the milk, vanilla, and several drops of food coloring. Stir the icing until it becomes a beautiful ocean blue. You may need to add a bit more milk or powdered sugar to get the right consistency for frosting.

Ocean Cookies Sequence Cards

Invite children to color the sequence cards. Then help them cut the cards apart. Allow children to use the cards for an independent sequencing activity.

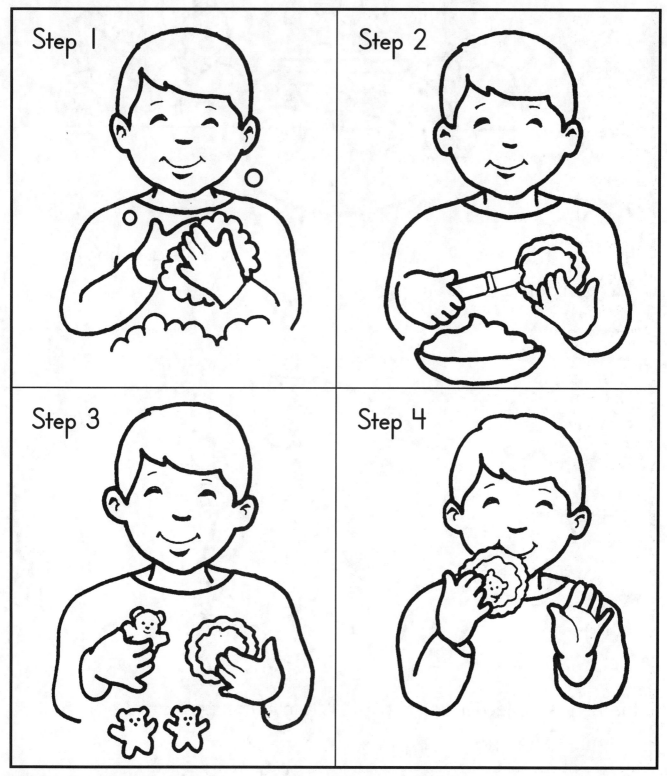

Beautiful Betta Fish

Our class has a new pet. It is a fish. It lives in a fishbowl in our classroom.

This fish is called a betta fish. Male betta fish are very colorful. They have long fins.

Beautiful Betta Fish *(cont.)*

Betta fish that live in the wild are found in small, dark waterholes.

They jump from waterhole to waterhole.

Beautiful Betta Fish *(cont.)*

We must be careful never to fill our fishbowl to the top.

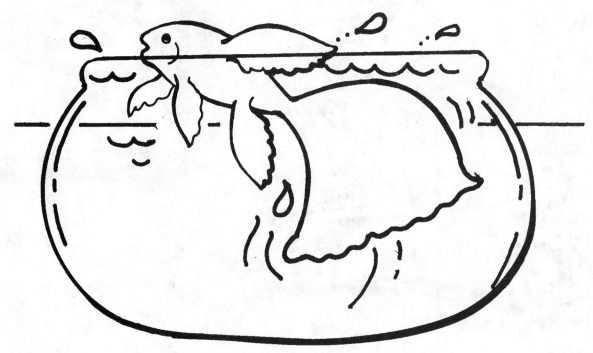

If we do, our betta fish could jump out!

Beautiful Betta Fish *(cont.)*

Bettas eat fish food. Each day a child in our class helps the teacher feed our fish.

All of the children are careful to give our betta just the right amount of food.

Beautiful Betta Fish (cont.)

We will be studying our betta fish and learning more about it.

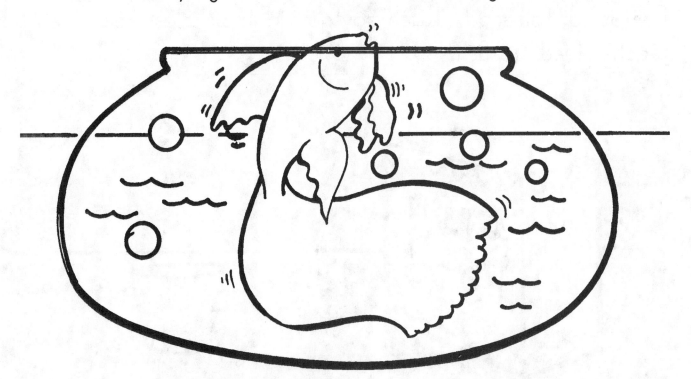

Here are two interesting facts I already know about bettas: These fish make bubble nests for their babies. Bettas can breathe air.

The Planets

Hands-On Internet Activities

Living Solar System Model

Trip to the Moon

Thematic Activities

Science—Felt Board Solar System

Cooking—Planet Pancakes

Storybook—Our Solar System

Annotated Web Sites

Planetary Picture List

http://www.anu.edu.au/Physics/nineplanets/picturelist.html

Begin your journey through space by learning about the planets in our solar system. This site offers a wide variety of links to various pictures of our solar system's planets and their moons.

NASA's Planetary Photojournal

http://photojournal.jpl.nasa.gov/

NASA has created a search engine for pictures of the solar system that allows you to locate pictures of specific planets and tells you which spacecraft or instrument photographed each image. For example, you can select the solar system as seen by Viking Orbiter 2. NASA states that this site has 1810 images with more being added each day.

NASA: A Space Library

http://samadhi.jpl.nasa.gov/

This NASA site is a virtual library of space information, including an awe-inspiring Solar System Simulator that allows you to decide where you are "standing" to view something else in the solar system. For example, you can "stand" on the moon and see a recently updated picture of the Earth as it would look from your vantage point on the moon. There are also interesting planetary surface maps, space artwork, and other fascinating space information.

Scientific America: A Parade of New Planets

http://www.sciam.com/explorations/052796explorations.html

Scientific America's site explores the up-to-date information about new planets that are being discovered outside of our solar system. Until recently, the idea that there were other planets was pure speculation. However, the fact that other planets did exist outside our solar system became a certainty when Michel Mayor and Didier Queloz of the Geneva Observatory detected a planet circling the star named 51 Pegasi.

Suggested Keyword Searches

planets, solar system, sun, Mercury, Venus, Earth, Mars, Jupiter, Saturn, Uranus, Neptune, Pluto, extrasolar planets, space shuttle, moon landing, astronauts, space travel, NASA

Living Solar System Model

Approximate Preparation Time

one hour

Learning Concept

Children use pictures of the planets printed from the Internet to make a living model of the solar system. This activity will help them increase their manual dexterity, science literacy and vocabulary, sequencing skills, ability to following directions, and cooperation skills.

Materials

- Our Solar System storybook (pages 40–50)
- classroom computer
- Internet Service Provider (ISP)
- bookmarked Web sites (page 33)
- computer printer
- printer paper

- laminator and laminating film or clear Contact™ paper
- poster board
- hole punch
- yarn

Lesson Preparation

Preview and bookmark Web sites that you intend to use with students. Make sure your printer is operational and that you have plenty of color ink.

At the Computer

Divide the class into small groups. Depending on the size of your class, assign one or more planets to each group. Make sure that one group is also assigned the sun. Allow time for each group to work at the computer. Ask students in a group to find their favorite picture of their assigned planet(s). Then help the group print the picture(s).

At Circle Time

To give children some background information about the planets, begin this unit by reading aloud the big book version of Our Solar System (pages 40–50). Make placards by gluing the planet pictures onto separate pieces of poster board. Then laminate or cover them with clear Contact™ paper. Punch two holes at the top of each piece of poster board. String a length of thick yarn through the holes and tie knots in the ends. Have children wear the placards. Arrange children in the order of the planets with the sun in the middle. Have children walk around in circles to demonstrate how the planets orbit the sun. Let children wear different placards and try again. Be sure that every child has an opportunity to participate. You may wish to take photographs of this activity to scan into your computer.

What to Say

First we are going to go online and find pictures of the planets and print them. Then we will need to make our pictures into planet placards that we can hang around our necks. (Model how a placard is hung around the neck.) Finally we will stand in the order that the planets orbit around the sun. Then we will walk in circles around the "sun" to see how the planets move.

Trip to the Moon

Approximate Preparation Time

two hours

Learning Concept

Children learn about the first moon landing, create a classroom spacecraft, and pretend to take a journey to the moon. This will help them increase their science literacy and vocabulary, as well as enhance ability to participate in creative dramatics.

Materials

- classroom computer
- Internet Service Provider (ISP)
- bookmarked Web sites (page 33)
- Space Helmet (page 36), one for each child
- crayons or markers
- big appliance box, several chairs, or a blanket hanging over a table (optional)

Lesson Preparation

Preview and bookmark a couple of Web sites that have historical moon landing information. Some things you may wish to locate for them are photos or pictures of the moon, various spacecraft, spacesuits, Earth as seen from the moon, and sound bytes of recorded landing tapes.

Reproduce the Space Helmet for children.

Circle Time

Give children a brief history of the moon landing. Discuss what happened, who was involved, and what it was like to be alive during that time. Talk with children about making a classroom spacecraft and pretending to land on the moon. Give children copies of the Space Helmet black line master. Encourage children to color their helmets. Build a classroom spacecraft using a big appliance box, a special arrangement of chairs, or a blanket hanging over a table. As an alternative to building a spacecraft, have children sit on the floor and pretend.

At the Computer

Have children view the bookmarked moon landing sites.

What to Say

In 1969, which is long before you were born, the United States sent some astronauts to the moon. Does anyone know what they went in? (Lead students to conclude that the astronauts traveled in a spacecraft.) I have bookmarked some interesting Web sites about the moon landing. Let's look at those now. Then we will make classroom spacecraft. After our spacecraft is done, we can pretend that we are astronauts and take an imaginary trip to the moon.

Space Helmet

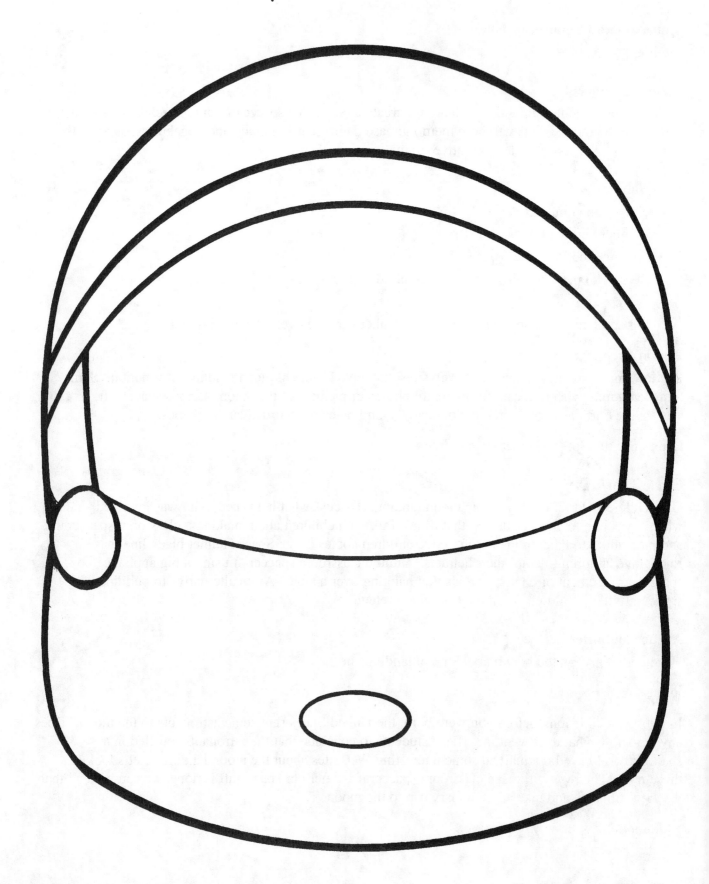

Felt Board Solar System

Approximate Preparation Time

30 minutes

Learning Concept

Children become familiar with the names and positions of the planets in our solar system. This activity enhances basic science literacy and improves fine motor coordination, shape recognition, and sequencing skills.

Materials

- Our Solar System storybook (pages 40–50)
- felt board or small cork bulletin board covered with a piece of felt
- easel (optional)

- felt
- scissors
- glue
- pictures of planets (page 34)

Lesson Preparation

Begin this activity by setting up your felt board. If you don't have a felt board, it is easy to make one by covering an old bulletin board with a piece of felt. Place the felt board on an easel or chair. Use the pictures of the planets that you have printed from the Internet for the activity on page 34 as guides to draw and cut simplified felt versions of the planets.

Directed Teaching Focus

Make time every morning during this unit to talk about the names and positions of the planets as you place the felt planets on the felt board.

Self-Directed Activity

Let children use the felt board and felt planets. Have them try to name the planets as they put the felt pieces in solar system order on the felt board.

What to Say

As you all know we are learning about the planets. We have read a storybook about the planets and seen some pictures of the planets on the Internet. Now we are going to use a felt board to see if we can put felt planets in the order of the real planets in our solar system. The planets in our solar system move around a star called the sun. Let's place the sun in the middle of the felt board. Then we can place the planets in the order they orbit, or circle, around the sun.

Technology Take-Off Point

Check to see if your version of Netscape Navigator or Internet Explorer allows you to save the bookmarks specified in the Annotated Web Sites so that they can be accessed without being connected to the Internet. This will give children a chance to click on the planet bookmarks while you are offline. Even though only the first Web page of any site will appear, this is an interesting and safe way for children to have time on the computer.

Planet Pancakes

Approximate Preparation Time

one hour

Learning Concept

By making these tempting Planet Pancakes children will improve their ability to listen to and follow directions, small-motor coordination, and sequencing skills.

Materials

- large electric frying pan or portable griddle (for adult use only)
- paper plates
- plastic utensils
- paper napkins or paper towels
- pancake recipe and ingredients (page 39)
- pancake syrup
- colored sprinkles
- crayons or markers

Warnings: Ask parents if their children have any food allergies or dietary restrictions. Never allow children near the hot frying pan or griddle or to handle anything that is hot.

Lesson Preparation

Set up a Cooking Center with the recipe and ingredients for making pancakes along with pancake syrup, and colored sprinkles. Arrange children's seating so that the lesson can be presented to the whole class or small groups. You may wish to enlist the help of volunteers. Remember to reproduce the recipe for the class cookbook and for student cookbooks that will be sent home at the end of the year.

Directed Teaching Focus

Talk about the planets as you make the pancakes. Have each child name the planet that he/she would like his/her pancake to look like. Invite children to tell what they know about the planets they have chosen for their pancakes.

Self-Directed Activity

Allow children to color their copies of the recipe.

What to Say

Since we have been learning a lot about the planets, today we are going to make pancakes that look like planets. You will help me make the pancake batter. Then each of you will choose your favorite planet. I will try to make a pancake that looks like the planet you have chosen.

Technology Take-Off Point

Check out the International House of Pancakes Web site at:

http://www.ihop.com/

The children's game room has a click-and-drag puzzle that youngsters can use to practice their mouse skills.

Recipe

Planet Pancakes

Ingredients

2 cups (500 mL) flour

4 teaspoons (20 mL) baking powder

1/2 teaspoon (2.5 mL) salt

2 eggs, beaten

2 cups (500 mL) milk

2 teaspoons (10 mL) melted butter

food coloring (optional)

Directions

In a bowl, combine the flour, baking powder, and salt. Add the beaten eggs, milk, and melted butter to the dry ingredients. Mix thoroughly. Pour some batter on the hot griddle or frying pan. Make the pancakes look like different planets, including a ring for Saturn. You may wish to add food coloring to change the color of the batter for the different planets.

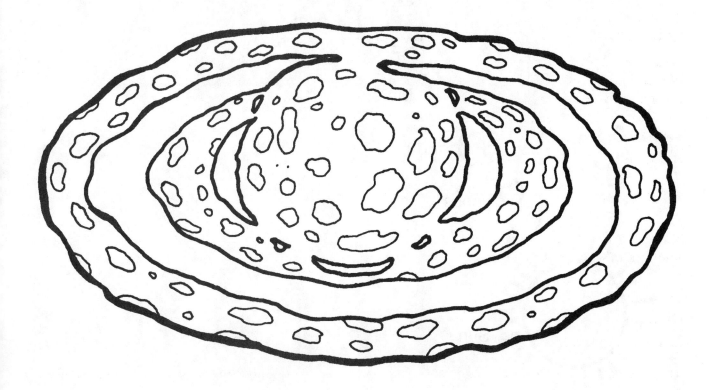

Our Solar System

We are learning about our solar system. Our solar system has one sun and nine planets. The nine planets in our solar system are Mercury, Venus, Earth, Mars, Jupiter, Saturn, Uranus, Neptune, and Pluto.

O Pluto

O Neptune

O Uranus

 Saturn

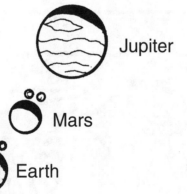 Jupiter

Mars

Earth

Venus

Mercury

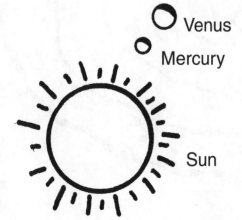 Sun

Our Solar System *(cont.)*

The center of our solar system is the sun. The sun is a star.

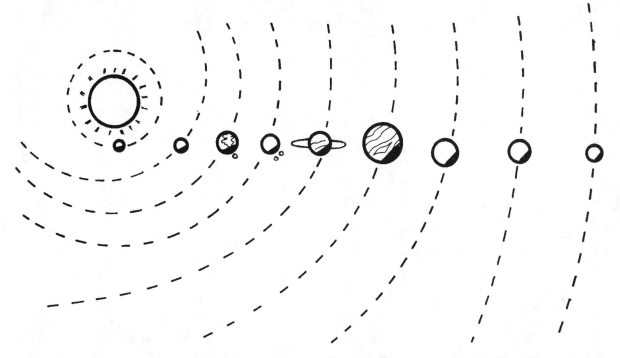

The nine planets move around the sun in an orbit. Each planet has its own orbit around the sun. Most planets have moons that orbit around the planet.

Our Solar System *(cont.)*

Mercury is the planet closest to the sun. Do you think you would feel hot or cold on Mercury? If you said hot, you are right. Mercury is so hot that nothing can live there. Mercury does not have a moon.

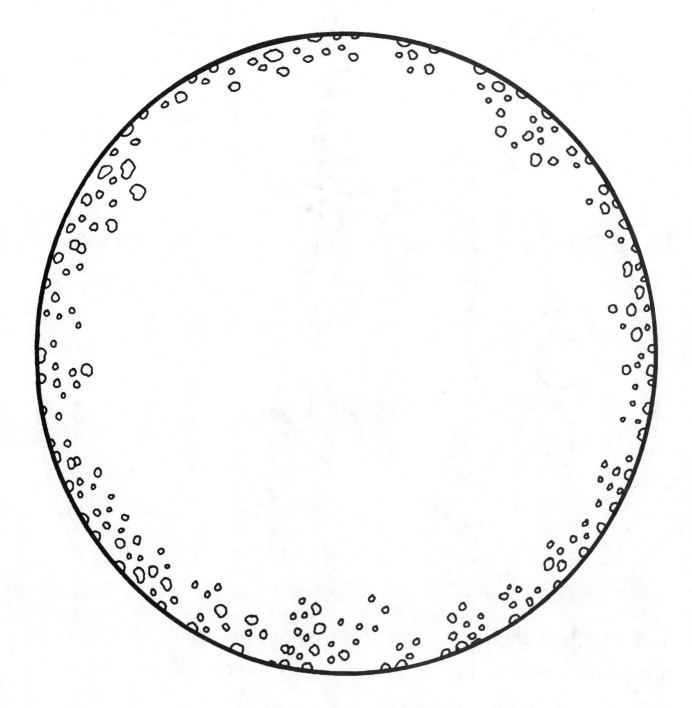

Our Solar System *(cont.)*

This picture shows Venus, the planet that is second from the sun. Venus is about the same size as Earth. Scientists do not believe that anything lives on Venus. In the night sky, Venus often shines brightly. It is sometimes called the morning star. Venus does not have a moon.

Our Solar System *(cont.)*

The third planet from the sun is Earth. That is where we live.
Many people, plants, and animals live on Earth. Earth has
one moon that can usually be seen shining in the night sky.

Our Solar System (cont.)

Mars is the fourth planet from the sun. It is the planet closest to Earth. Mars is sometimes called the Red Planet. Can you guess why? If you said that it looks red, you are right.

Scientists have sent spaceships with machines to explore Mars. The machines took pictures that showed the dirt and rocks on Mars are red. Mars has two moons.

Our Solar System *(cont.)*

The fifth planet from the sun is Jupiter. Jupiter is the giant of our solar system. This planet has striped bands and a big red spot. Scientists think the spot is a storm that has lasted for hundreds of years. Jupiter has 16 moons. What do you think it would be like to look up in the night sky and see 16 moons?

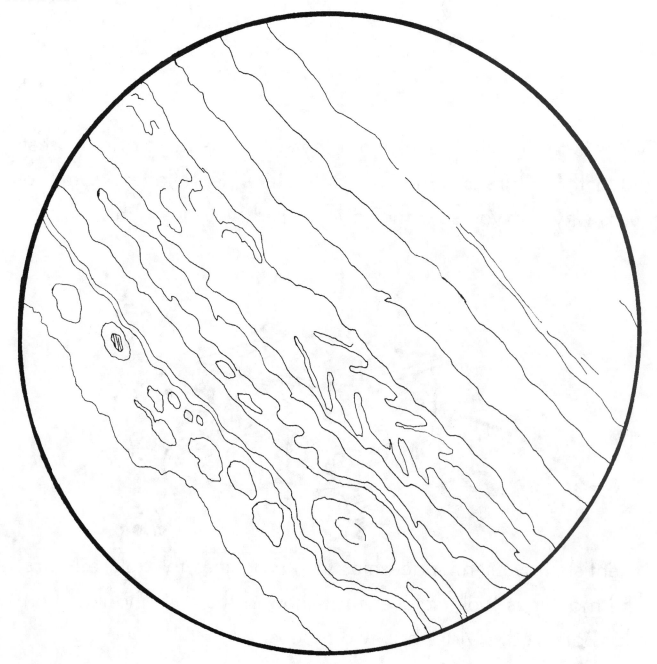

Our Solar System *(cont.)*

Saturn is the sixth planet from the sun. What can you tell about Saturn from this picture? If you said Saturn has rings, you are right. The rings are made mostly of little pieces of ice. Saturn has 18 moons.

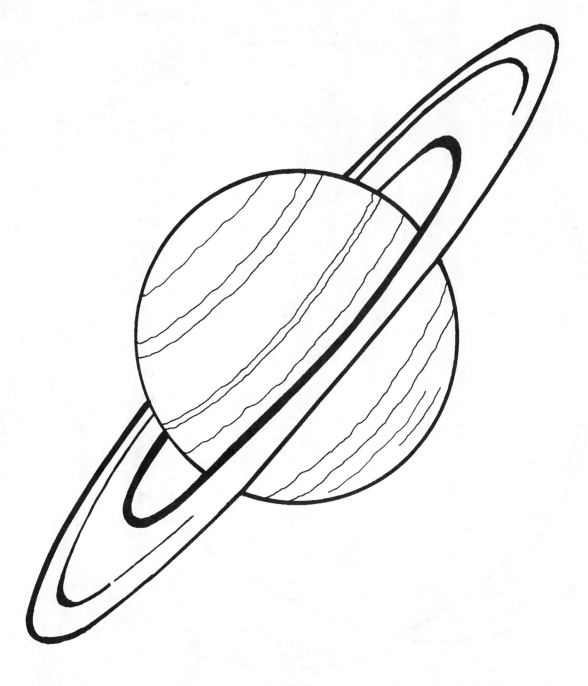

Our Solar System *(cont.)*

The seventh planet is Uranus. Uranus is very far away from the sun. Like Saturn, Uranus has a ring around it and 18 moons. Would it be hot or cold on Uranus? Brrr! You're right if you said it would be very cold.

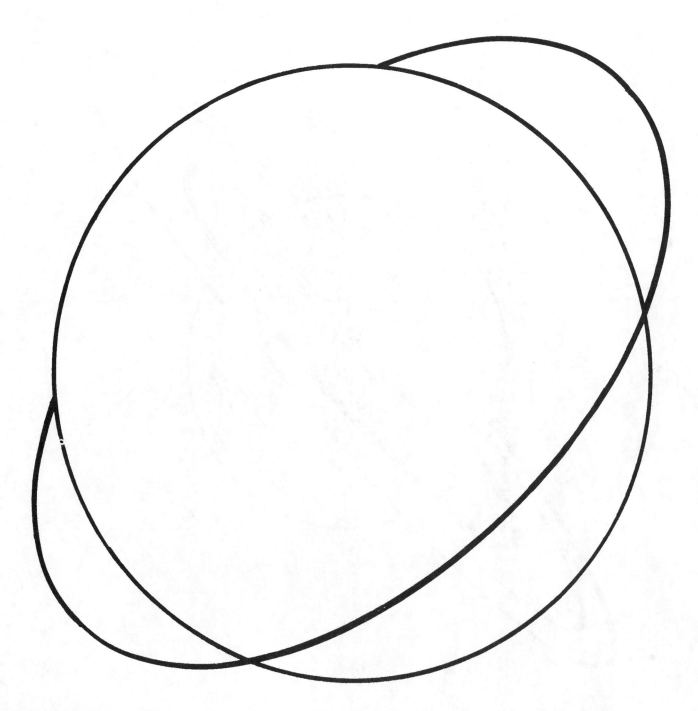

Our Solar System *(cont.)*

Neptune is the eighth planet from the sun. Neptune has rings and eight moons.

Our Solar System *(cont.)*

The ninth and last planet in our solar system is Pluto. Pluto is the coldest planet. We don't know very much about this planet because it is very far away. Pluto has one moon.

Planet Earth Membership Certificate

My name is _____.

I live on the planet Earth.

The thing I like best about living on Earth is _____

_____.

Teacher: _____ Date: _____

The Earth and Sky

Hands-On Internet Activities

E-mail Weather Reports

Digital Weather Pictures

Thematic Activities

Science—Making a Mini-Greenhouse

Art—Making a Windsock

Cooking—Jelly Bean Gardens

Storybook—Little Flower's Happy Day

Annotated Web Sites

Observing Clouds

http://athena.wednet.edu/curric/weather/pricloud/index.html

This is a small, simple, and very visually appealing site that shows beautiful photographs of the three basic types of clouds and includes descriptions of each.

MonarchWatch

http://www.monarchwatch.org/

This site is dedicated to Monarch butterflies. There is butterfly gardening and life cycle information, monarch posters, classroom guides, tons of pictures, and inexpensive kits that you can order for students to raise their own butterflies.

Volcano World

http://volcano.und.nodak.edu/vwdocs/kids/kids.html

The Kids' Door section of Volcano World is a multimedia site that you can use to introduce children to volcanoes. There are virtual tours of several volcanoes on Earth and one on Mars. Volcano World has a section of artwork submitted by students. Some of the online games may be a little advanced for very young children.

Pitara for Kids

http://www.pitara.com/earth/earth.asp

Pitara for Kids is a well-rounded resource for early childhood educators to use in their classrooms. Pitara's section about Earth has a great deal of information about animals, volcanoes, tornadoes, insects, planets, and plants. It is very kid-friendly and a great place to go for generating ideas.

Suggested Keyword Searches

earth, clouds, weather, monarch butterflies, volcano, tornado, animals, plants, insects (You may also wish to search for specific types of weather, animals, plants, insects, and other kinds of butterflies.)

E-mail Weather Reports

Approximate Preparation Time

several hours

Learning Concept

Children gain hands-on computer experience while determining the local weather and sending a picture weather report to an e-mail pen pal. This activity enhances earth science vocabulary and literacy.

Materials

- classroom computer
- Internet Service Provider (ISP)
- e-mail account
- bookmarked Web sites (page 52)
- computer printer
- printer paper
- weather pictures from clip art software or downloaded from the Internet
- word processing software (if you are using the clip art method)
- e-mail pen pal
- poster board
- markers

Lesson Preparation

Preview and bookmark Web sites that you intend to use with students. Select pictures using clip art and/or images downloaded from the Internet. See Saving Images and Pictures to Disk (page 304) for additional information.

First you must find an Internet pen pal. See Locating E-Mail Pen Pals on page 55 and the Sample E-Mail Pen Pal Inquiry on page 56. Revise the letter according to your needs.

Make a class chart to keep track of the weather every day. Set up your Computer Center to be a weather station.

Class Weather Chart		
Date	**Type of Weather**	**Temperature**

Clip Art Weather Pictures

Check the clip art you currently have on your computer. Most word processing software has a variety of clip art that might include weather pictures. You may wish to purchase a CD-ROM collection of clip art that is available from most computer stores. Create a word processor document for each weather picture. At the top of the document, label the type of weather that is shown in the picture. Then save the document using a name that makes the file easy to identify. For example, save a picture of a shining sun in a word processor document, label the picture "Sunny" using a large type size and easy-to-read font. Then save the document using the name *sunny*.

E-mail Weather Reports *(cont.)*

Downloading Weather Pictures

Downloading images from the Internet to your hard drive or disk is very simple on a PC using Microsoft Windows 95 or better or on a MAC using Microsoft Word. For a PC, you need to select a picture on a Web site and right click on it. This will make a floating menu appear. Select "Save as," name the file, and save the image to your hard drive or a disk. For a MAC, click and hold the mouse button until the floating menu appears. Then click "Save this image as," name the file, and save the image to your hard drive or a disk.

Circle Time

Talk to students about the different kinds of weather. At about the same time each day, take children outside to determine what kind of weather you are having. Teach children to identify the following weather conditions and temperatures: sunny, rainy, cloudy, snowy, hot, warm, cool, cold, and freezing. Have them record the information on the class weather chart.

At the Computer

Show children the pictures you have saved that show different kinds of weather. Ask them to decide what your weather is like that day. Have them pick a picture that they feel represents that type of weather.

Write a simple e-mail message—such as "Guess what our weather is like today!"—to your pen pal. Add the weather picture that students have chosen as an e-mail attachment. Encourage your e-mail pen pal to send daily weather reports to your class.

What to Say

Today we are going to send our e-mail pen pal our weather report. Before we do, we have to figure out what kind of weather we are having. (Take children outside to see what the weather is like. Then return to the classroom.) Who wants to report the weather today? (Select a student to tell what kind of weather you are having.) Let's go find a picture of sunny weather to send our pen pal. (Show and read aloud the file names for the different types of weather pictures that you have saved. Encourage children to pick one picture that depicts the type of weather you are having that day.) Now I will type our pen pal's e-mail address and a message. (Type in the e-mail address and the message, "Guess what our weather is like today!" Read this information aloud as you type it.) I will attach the picture file to the e-mail. This means that we are sending our weather picture with our letter. When our pen pal opens the attached picture file, he/she will see the weather picture we have sent. Then our pen pal will know what kind of weather we are having here today.

Locating E-Mail Pen Pals

WARNING: Open all e-mail during lesson preparation time without students being there. If the content is appropriate, view it again with children.

There are a variety of ways to get children involved in e-mail communications with pen pals.

 Set up two e-mail mailboxes, one for yourself and one for the class. Some Internet Service Providers will allow you to have a second mailbox without an additional charge. Once you have two mailboxes, have children send e-mail to your address. Then you can e-mail responses to the children's address.

 Invite parents to become e-mail pen pals for your class.

 Encourage teachers in your school to be e-mail pen pals or to have their students be e-mail pen pals for your class.

 Invite teachers at other local schools to be e-mail pen pals. Often older children enjoy corresponding with younger ones. However, make sure that an adult will be monitoring the content of e-mails being sent to your class.

 Ask experts that you contact on the Internet if they will correspond with your class.

 Invite faculty members or students at a local college or university to be e-mail pen pals with your class.

 Ask a local business to take part in your e-mail pen pal activity. Many large organizations devote a certain amount of time and funds to supporting local schools.

 Talk to educators at meetings for professional organizations about being e-mail pen pals. Make sure to network by giving out your e-mail address to those who are interested in participating.

 Find pen pals online. As you peruse Web sites, e-mail those involved with a particular site.

 Try some or all of the following pen pal sites.

Cyberkids—pen pal service for children who are age six or older
http://studybuddy.com/connect/cyberkids/index.html

Epals—classroom pen pals from 100 countries around the world
http://www.epals.com/

AlphaBits—pen pals for Canadian children
http://204.50.57.45/penpal.html

All About Education—a pen pal site for educators and children
http://www.vsns.com/aae/

Sample E-Mail Pen Pal Inquiry

Hello,

My name is _____. I am an
(first and last name)

early childhood teacher at _____
(name of school)

in _____ .
(city, state)

The children I teach range in age from _____ to _____.
(age range)

I am using the Internet as a learning tool in my preschool classroom. I am looking for people who are interested in becoming e-mail pen pals for my students. This would involve receiving e-mails from our class and responding to them on a regular basis.

Our first activity for which we need e-mail pen pals is a weather project. We will send you a picture that shows what our local weather is like. After you receive our e-mail, we would like you to tell us what your weather is like. You can send us a picture or just type it in an e-mail.

Please let me know if you would like to do this, share suggestions about how would work, or suggest any other Internet collaboration ideas you would like to try. I look forward to your response.

Sincerely,

_____
Teacher

_____
School

_____
E-mail Address

Digital Weather Pictures

Approximate Preparation Time

two hours

Learning Concept

This activity is an extension of or alternative to E-mail Weather Reports (pages 53 and 54). Children help take daily weather photographs that they e-mail to their weather pen pals. This activity increases young children's fine-motor coordination and mouse skills and enhances their earth science vocabulary and literacy.

Materials

- classroom computer
- Internet Service Provider (ISP)
- digital camera or regular camera with film developed to CD-ROM
- props, such as clothing and accessories, for different kinds of weather

Lesson Preparation

Obtain a digital camera or a regular camera and film. Have children bring props, such as clothing and accessories, for different kinds of weather. Examples include umbrella, sunglasses, sun hat, knit cap, and mittens. Some of these items may be purchased at thrift shops, or you may wish to enlist the help of parents to collect them.

If you take pictures with a regular camera, you will need to have them developed onto a CD-ROM before you can put them on your computer. If you take pictures with a digital camera, you will be ready to transfer those digital pictures to your computer. Read the user's manual that came with the digital camera to learn how to store the images on your computer hard drive.

Circle and Center Time

Scout the school grounds with children and decide where to take a simple weather picture to show what the weather is like. First discuss with children what the weather is like that day. Then work together to plan the photograph. Have children make use of props that help convey the type of weather it is.

At the Computer

Each day let children watch you open the computer file with the appropriate weather photograph, create the e-mail, and attach the weather photograph. After children have observed many times, let them use the mouse to select the address from the address book, select the weather photograph, send the e-mail, etc.

What to Say

We are going to take a photograph of today's weather. We will put the picture on our computer and send it to our e-mail pen pals. Since it is sunny, let's go outside and find a place where we can take a picture that shows that it is sunny here. What kinds of props should we use to show that it is sunny? (Encourage children to name props that would help show it is sunny weather.)

Making a Mini-Greenhouse

Approximate Preparation Time

one hour

Learning Concept

Children explore plants as they create their own mini-greenhouses and watch seeds grow. This activity enhances children's basic science literacy and vocabulary, as well as improves their ability to follow directions, observe changes over time, and understand the life cycle of plants.

Materials

- empty, clear plastic liter or quart bottles, one for each child
- potting soil
- seeds
- utility knife (for adult use only)
- wide masking tape
- permanent black marker
- water
- watering can or small container for pouring water
- My Plant Growth Record (page 60), several copies for each child
- Little Flower's Happy Day storybook (pages 66–73)

Lesson Preparation

Prepare for this activity by gathering the materials that you need. You may wish to ask parents to help you collect empty, clear plastic liter or quart bottles. If so, be sure to notify them ahead of time.

Preparation for Each Bottle

Note: Have children help with as many steps as possible.

Warning: The utility knife is for adult use only.

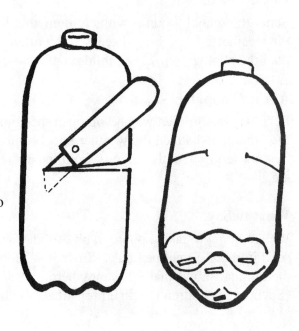

1. Clean and dry the plastic bottle.
2. Remove any labels that are on the bottle.
3. Keep the cap screwed on the top of the bottle.
4. Use a utility knife to cut around the middle of the bottle about 3/4 of the way. Be sure to leave a section of the bottle uncut so that the top half is still connected to the bottom half. This will allow you to open and close the greenhouse.
5. Use the utility knife to poke several slits in the bottom of each bottle. This will allow excess water to drain out of the greenhouse.

Making a Mini-Greenhouse *(cont.)*

Planting Procedure for Each Greenhouse

Note: Have children help with as many steps as possible.

Warning: The utility knife is for adult use only.

1. Open the top of the greenhouse so that the upper half of the bottle is pulled all the way back.
2. Place two cups of potting soil in the bottom of the greenhouse.
3. With a finger, hollow out a hole in the soil and place the seeds in the hole.
4. Cover the seeds with soil.
5. Water gently.
6. Close the greenhouse and use masking tape to seal it along the cut line. Be sure to write children's names on the taped portion of their greenhouses with a permanent black marker.
7. Water the plant as needed by removing the cap of the bottle.

Directed Teaching Focus

Read aloud the storybook Little Flower's Happy Day. Discuss how a plant grows from a seed. Talk about recycling. Tell children that you are recycling the plastic containers used for the greenhouses. When children's seedlings are at least 3" (8 cm) high, cut off the top of the greenhouse. Show how the greenhouse is now a planter. You may wish to have children decorate the planter with ribbon and give the seedling as a gift.

Self-Directed Activity

Have children check their plant each day during Center Time. Have them draw a picture of their plant using My Plant Growth Record (page 60). Each child should make a sequence of drawings to show what their plants look like as it grows. Send the drawings and the plant home with children.

What to Say

We have been learning about plants. First we read a little storybook about how a plant started out as a little seed, became a seedling, then a little plant, then a little flower. Now I am going to help you make little greenhouses and plant seeds in them. Each of you will have your own greenhouse and plant to take care of. Each day you will look at your plant to see how it has changed. Then you will draw a picture to show what you plant looks like.

Technology Take-Off Point

The Environmental Protection Agency (EPA) has a wonderful site with many features that can be used to introduce children to protecting the environment in an age-appropriate way. Consider using some of the hands-on games. There is one in which children are asked to pick pictures that show people doing something that harms the environment. This game is appealing and informative even for young children. In addition, there is a coloring book that you can download. However, it requires Adobe Reader. If you do not already have Adobe Reader, this site allows you to download and install it. The address for the Web site follows:

http://www.epa.gov/kids/

My Plant Growth Record

Name: _____   Date: _____

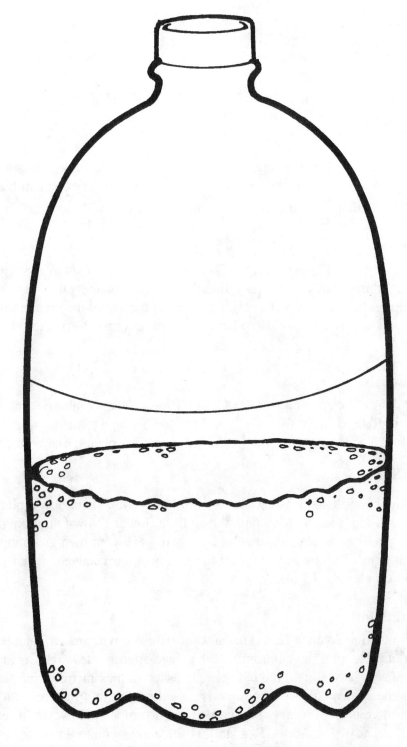

This is how my plant looks today.

Making a Windsock

Approximate Preparation Time

30 minutes

Learning Concept

In this activity young children learn about the wind and how it makes objects move by creating this colorful, easy-to-make windsock. This activity improves fine motor coordination and listening skills.

Materials

- construction paper (various colors)
- glue or glue stick
- glitter
- blunt children's scissors

- crepe paper
- stapler and staples
- hole punch
- yarn

Lesson Preparation

Prepare for this activity setting up an Art Center with the materials needed for this project. It is a good idea to use this art experience after you have had time to do some of the other activities in this unit, including the hands-on Internet experiences.

Directed Teaching Focus

Talk with children about the wind. Walk outside together and see if they can feel the wind. Show them how to lick a finger and hold it up to see they can feel the wind. Notice if the wind is blowing the trees or moving your flag. Then move back inside the classroom to make the windsocks.

Model the following directions for children. Have them complete a step after you model it. Provide help as needed.

1. Fold the construction paper in half so that it looks like a book.

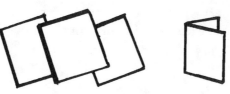

2. Cut across the fold making 1" (2.5 cm) wide strips and leaving about 2" (5 cm) at the top uncut.

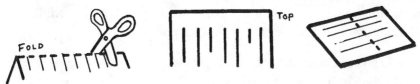

3. Unfold the paper. Lay it flat with the fold line facing up. Glue glitter onto the strips. Allow the glue to dry. Shake off any excess glitter.

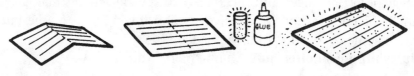

Making a Windsock *(cont.)*

4. Hold the paper like an open book. Roll the corners together to create a tube with the fold in the middle. The cut strips should open up to look like a paper lantern. Staple the ends of the windsock to hold the tube in place.

  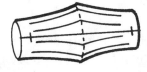

5. Cut long crepe paper strips. Use staples to attach one end of each crepe paper strip to the inside bottom of the windsock. (It does not matter which end you pick to be the bottom of the windsock.)

6. Punch two holes on opposite sides at the top of the windsock. String a piece of yarn through each hole. Tie knots to secure the yarn in place.

7. Hang the windsock outside near a classroom window by knotting together the loose ends of yarn.

Self-Directed Activity

Ask children to check the windsocks each day. During your weather report, ask them to tell you whether there is any wind.

What to Say

Let's go outside to see if we can tell whether there is any wind today. If there is wind, how will we know? (Ask volunteers to suggest ways that it is possible to tell when the wind is blowing.) Let's go look. (Take the children outside to explore the wind conditions.)

Now let's go back inside so we can make windsocks. A windsock is a weather instrument that is used to see if it is windy. If it is windy, our windsock will move.

Technology Take-Off Point

Hoffer Elementary School in Banning, California, is one of several schools that has worked under the direction of the Franklin Science Institute to create and publish wind units on the Internet. Check out this school's interesting home page at the following address:
http://cmp1.ucr.edu/exhibitions/hoffer/hoffer.home page.html

Jelly Bean Gardens

Approximate Preparation Time

30 minutes

Learning Concept

Use this activity as an opportunity to talk about flowers, gardens, and the sun. Children learn to follow directions in sequential order.

Materials

- small jelly beans
- candy sticks, at least one per child
- small plastic or paper bowls or baby food jars, one for each child
- Jelly Bean Garden Flowers (page 64), one copy for every twelve children

- tape
- scissors
- crayons
- pipe cleaners

Warning: Ask parents if their children have any food allergies or dietary restrictions.

Lesson Preparation

Gather the materials listed above and place them in an Art Center. Reproduce the Jelly Bean Garden Flowers so that each child can make one or more flowers.

Directed Teaching Focus

Discuss plant growth. Talk about how these candy flowers compare to real flowers. Have children color and cut out one or more paper flowers. Put their initials on the backs of their flowers. Help them tape each flower to the top of a candy stick. Let each child fill a bowl with jelly beans and poke the candy stick into them. Make sure the shape of the bowl you are using will allow the flowers to stand upright when they are placed in the jelly beans. In general, the higher the sides of the bowl, the easier the flowers will stand.

Self-Directed Activity

Put pipe cleaners and the paper flowers in your Art Center so children can make more pretend flowers whenever they have free time.

What to Say

We have been learning about how things grow. We have learned that flowers need sunshine and water to bloom. Today we are going to make a pretend flower garden. These flowers don't need water or sunshine because they are candy flowers.

Technology Take-Off Point

To find links for information and a variety of child-pleasing ideas, go to the National Confectioners Association Web site at the following address:

http://www.kidscandy.org

Jelly Bean Garden Flowers

Jelly Bean Flowers Recipe

Jelly Bean Flowers

Materials

1/2 cup (100 g) jelly beans

1 candy sticks

1 small plastic or paper bowl

1 paper flower

tape

scissors

crayons

Directions

Fill the bowl with jelly beans. Tape a paper flower to each candy stick. Plant the garden by putting the stick flower in the jelly bean bowl.

Little Flower's Happy Day

Over the lonely hill there was a little green valley. The little valley was covered in grass that grew like a carpet of green velvet. It was a lovely little valley.

66

Little Flower's Happy Day *(cont.)*

Every morning the sun rose. The sun would always smile cheerfully at the little valley and say, "Good morning!" The little valley smiled back at the shining sun.

The leaves on the trees glittered, and the beautiful grass twinkled like a million green stars.

Little Flower's Happy Day (cont.)

One day something happened in the little valley. A tiny plant began to grow. At first the plant was just a little seed. It was warm and cozy in the earth, wrapped up like a little baby in a blanket.

Little Flower's Happy Day (cont.)

The sun shined all through the day in the little valley. Soon the little seed began to feel like stretching. After a while, the little seed wanted to stick her little head out of the earth's warm blanket to look around. And so she did.

Little Flower's Happy Day *(cont.)*

The wonderful sunshine made her feel like stretching even more. As she stretched and stretched, she grew and grew. Before long the tiny little seedling became a tiny plant.

Now that she was a little bit taller, she could see over the blades of grass. "Isn't this lovely!" she thought as she looked at her beautiful home in the little valley.

70

Little Flower's Happy Day *(cont.)*

One afternoon the little plant couldn't see the sun. She wondered why. Suddenly a sprinkle of water fell upon her tiny head. "That's odd," she said. "I wonder where this water is coming from?"

"Up here, little plant!" giggled a cute cloud. "I am raining on you! Doesn't it feel good?" said the cloud.

"Yes, it does," said the little plant, "and I am thirsty." Then she used her roots that were in the warm blanket of earth to sip the water that fell from the cute cloud.

Little Flower's Happy Day (cont.)

Days passed. Suddenly, the little plant felt a tiny bump on her head. "I wonder what that is?" she asked as she strained to look up. "Mister Tree, I have a bump on my head. Can you see what it is?"

"Yes, my dear, it's a bud. One day soon you are going to have a flower!" said the tree.

"A flower! How exciting!" said the little plant.

Little Flower's Happy Day *(cont.)*

A few days later a wonderful thing happened. When the little plant awoke, she felt strange, yet somehow more beautiful. Yes, she had bloomed. She had become a little flower.

The little flower beamed with pride. Her friends—the sun, the cloud, the tree, and the grass—all exclaimed that her flower was the most beautiful one they had ever seen. And it was.

"Oh, what a happy day," said the little flower. "This is my happiest day ever! From this day on I will call myself Little Flower!" And that is how Little Flower had her happy day.

Animals

Hands-On Internet Activities

Ask the Zookeeper
Alphabet Zoo

Thematic Activities

Art—Hanging Snake
Cooking—Bow-Wow in a Blankie
Storybook—A Visit to the Zoo

Annotated Web Sites

The Birmingham Zoo

http://www.birminghamzoo.com/

Internet zoos are the next best thing to being there. There is a wealth of information on this site. The Animal Omnibus portion of the site, according to its creators, "…is a list of Web sources indexed by the name of the animal." As you look for sites with pictures of animals to bookmark, this is an excellent starting point. In addition to pictures, this site also has movies showing the daily lives of real animals at the Birmingham Zoo, free screensaver downloads, coloring pages, and much more.

Sounds of the World's Animals

http://www.georgetown.edu/cball/animals/animals.html

Learning to make animal noises is one of the joys of being a young child. This site has animal photos and presents the animals sounds as they are interpreted in a variety of languages. Learn how people who speak other languages bark, meow, moo, etc.

St. Louis Zoo

http://www.stlzoo.org/home.asp

This Web site includes a children's section that introduces youngsters to new zoo babies, offers printable coloring pages, and has an online animal adoption program, as well as many other features. There is a teachers' section that offers newsletters, networking meetings, and a materials lending library for educators in the greater St. Louis metro area.

San Diego Zoo

http://www.sandiegozoo.org/

The San Diego Zoo is one of the most famous zoos and animal parks in the world. Its Web site features a multitude of options, including electronic postcards that you can send for free.

Suggested Keyword Searches

zoo, animals (You may also wish to search for the specific names of zoos or specific types of animals.)

Ask the Zookeeper

Approximate Preparation Time

one hour

Learning Concept

Having children formulate questions to e-mail to a real zookeeper helps them increase their science literacy and vocabulary, oral language skills, and reading readiness skills.

Materials

- classroom computer
- Internet Service Provider (ISP)
- bookmarked Web sites (page 74)
- A Visit to the Zoo storybook (pages 82–90)

- e-mail account
- computer printer
- printer paper
- three-ring binder

Lesson Preparation

Preview and bookmark Web sites that you intend to use with students.

At the Computer

Explore the zoo sites you have found. You may wish to take advantage of downloading some of the movies available on the Birmingham Zoo Web site. Write down the questions children ask as they see the animals on the Web sites. Make sure children get enough information to be able to ask questions. To send the questions, click on the zookeeper hyperlink. A hyperlink is the text or image that is programmed to connect you to another page or link. If it is text, a hyperlink is often in another color than the main body of information. When you position your mouse arrow over a hyperlink, a pointer hand appears on the screen. A blank e-mail form should appear. If this doesn't happen, here's what to do. Open your e-mail program. Then, on a PC, highlight the e-mail address, press Ctrl + C to copy the address, place the cursor in the e-mail address textbox, and press Ctrl + V to paste the address in the correct place. On a MAC, highlight the e-mail address, press the apple key and C to copy the address, place the cursor in the e-mail address textbox, and press the apple key and V to paste the address in the correct place.

Circle Time

Read aloud A Visit to the Zoo. After visiting some Internet zoos, brainstorm with children questions they would like to ask a zookeeper. Discuss with children what they have seen on the Internet and help them agree on several specific questions to ask a zookeeper. General requests for information are usually just referred to a place on the Web site that provides an answer.

What to Say

We are going to use the Internet to learn about animals at some zoos. After we have looked at animal pictures and heard animal sounds, we are going to think of questions that we would like to ask a zookeeper. Then we are going to e-mail the questions to the zookeeper. The zookeeper will read our letter and send us an answer. This might take a few days, but we will check our e-mail every day to see if the zookeeper has sent us answers to our questions.

Alphabet Zoo

Approximate Preparation Time

one hour

Learning Concept

This activity reinforces letter recognition, vocabulary development, reading readiness skills, and science literacy.

Materials

- classroom computer
- computer printer
- three-ring binder
- alphabet page dividers (see below)

- Internet Service Provider (ISP)
- printer paper
- three-hole punch

Lesson Preparation

Preview and bookmark Web sites that you intend to use with students.

Make letter dividers for your binder using your word processing software to make a large (type size about 72 point) capital and lower case letter for each letter in the alphabet. If your word processing type sizes are not large enough, draw the letter dividers by hand. Be sure to make a separate page for each letter of the alphabet.

Circle Time

Introduce this alphabet activity at Circle Time by displaying the three-ring binder. Show children the large letter dividers. Read and recite the letters of the alphabet with children as you flip through the letter dividers. You may wish to brainstorm a list of animal names that start with each letter. See page 77 for some suggestions. After you have placed animal pictures in the binder, review the alphabet by naming the letter and the zoo animals whose names begin with that letter.

At the Computer

Each day lead your class through an Internet alphabet exploration by having children "hunt" for an animal with a name that starts with a specific letter. Encourage children to name the animals they see and identify the first letter of each animal name. When children have spotted an animal that begins with the correct letter, print the animal's picture, and add it to the correct section of the alphabet zoo binder. Print as many different animal pictures as you can for each letter.

What to Say

Today we are going to start making our own alphabet zoo book. To do this we are going to visit different Web sites on the Internet and see how many zoo animals we can find. First let's look at this book and say all the letters aloud. Let's talk about the first letter in the alphabet, the letter **a**. Today we are going to find a zoo animal with a name that begins with the letter **a**. Let's take a look at some zoo Web sites on the computer. (After finding and printing an animal picture for one letter, continue with the next letter of the alphabet.)

Suggested Animal List

Aa—aardvark, alligator, anaconda, anteater, antelope, ape

Bb—barn owl, bat, bear, bison, boa constrictor, bull

Cc—camel, chameleon, chimpanzee, cobra, cougar, crocodile

Dd—deer, dolphin, duck

Ee—eagle, eastern box turtle, egret, elephant, emu

Ff—fennec fox, ferret, field mouse, fish, flying dragon, frog

Gg— gazelle, gila monster, giraffe, goat, gorilla, great horned owl

Hh—hippopotamus, horned toad, horse, howler monkey, hyena

Ii—iguana, ibex

Jj—jackal, jaguar, joey

Kk—kangaroo, killer whale, kingfisher, koala, Komodo dragon

Ll—leafcutter ant, lemur, leopard, lion, llama

Mm—manatee, marmoset, meercat, monkey, moose, mouse

Nn—needlefish, night hawk, night heron, night owl

Oo—okapi, orangutan, oryx, ostrich, otter, owl

Pp—parrot, penguin, pigmy elephant, polar bear, python

Qq—quail

Rr—rabbit, raccoon, rattlesnake, reindeer, reptile, rhinoceros

Ss—sailfish, salamander, sandpiper, seal, skunk, sloth, snake

Tt—tamarin, tapir, tarantula, tiger, toucan, turtle

Uu—umbrella bird

Vv—vampire bat, vervet monkey, vulture

Ww—wallaby, walrus, warthog, weasel, white-tailed deer, wolf

Xx—xiphosuran (horseshoe crab)

Yy—yak

Zz—zebra

Hanging Snake

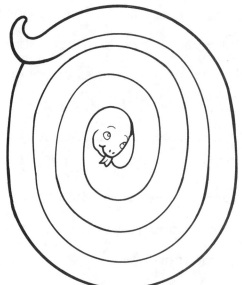

Approximate Preparation Time

30 minutes

Learning Concept

Children improve their listening skills and fine
motor coordination and increase their science vocabulary.

Materials

- Snake Pattern (page 79), one for each child and some extras
- cardstock
- scissors
- crayons
- hole punch
- yarn

Lesson Preparation

Preview and bookmark Web sites that you intend to use with students. Reproduce the snake pattern
onto cardstock, making one for each child plus a few extras.

Directed Teaching Focus

Begin by reminding children about the kinds of snakes they have studied on the Internet. Take another
look at the some snake pictures. Remember to reintroduce names and talk about the various defining
characteristics of the snakes. Talk with the class about real snakes that children have seen and discuss
what they looked like.

Have children color their snake patterns. Then help children cut out their patterns, cutting along the
interior solid line to make a spiral. Ask children what type of snakes they are making. Punch a hole in
one end of each snake. Thread a piece of yarn through the hole and gently tie a knot. Hang the snakes
around the classroom.

Self-Directed Activity

Place extra copies of the snake patterns in your Art Center for children to make more snakes when time
allows.

What to Say

Today we are going to make hanging snakes. Before we do, let's see if we can remember some things
that we have learned about snakes. Let's look at some Internet Web sites where there are interesting
pictures of snakes. (Show children pictures.) Color your snake. Then I will help you cut it out.
(Provide assistance as needed.

Technology Take-Off Point

Search Ask.com with questions about snakes and other reptiles. In addition, try the Electronic Zoo
page, which is devoted to snakes and reptiles, at the following address:

http://netvet.wustl.edu/reptiles.htm#snake

Snake Pattern

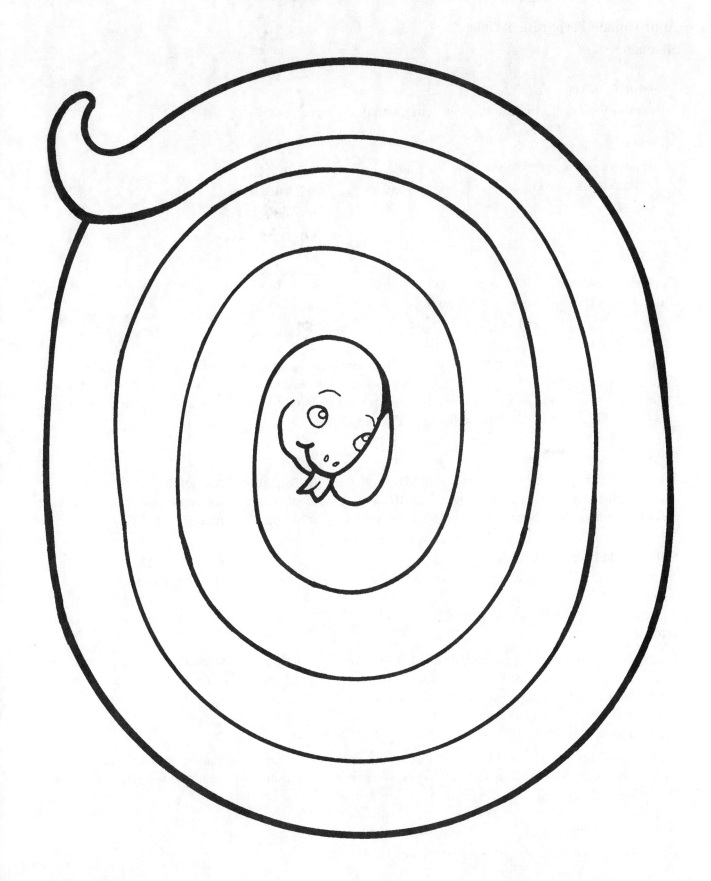

Bow-Wow in a Blankie

Approximate Preparation Time

30 minutes

Learning Concept

This activity enhances listening, sequencing, and oral language skills.

Materials

- ingredients and recipe for Bow-Wow in a Blankie (page 81)
- napkins
- paper plates
- metal spatula
- tongs
- toaster oven
- oven mitts
- paper towels

Warnings: Ask parents if their children have any food allergies or dietary restrictions. Never allow children near the hot toaster oven or to handle anything that is hot.

Lesson Preparation

Set up a Cooking Center with the recipe and ingredients for making Bow-Wow in a Blankie. Arrange children's seating so that the lesson can be presented to the whole class or small groups. You may wish to enlist the help of volunteers. Remember to reproduce the recipe for the class cookbook and for student cookbooks that will be sent home at the end of the year.

Directed Teaching Focus

Talk with children about the recipe and model how to do it. Talk about how hot dogs have a funny name and how they really aren't dogs at all. Research the history of the hot dog online to give children some fun facts. Talk about who invented hot dogs and how hot dogs are made.

Self-Directed Activity

Add the recipe master to your art center and allow children to color their own copy to add to their recipe booklet.

What to Say

Today we are going to make a recipe called Bow-Wow in a Blankie. (Discuss the ingredients and how the Bow-Wows are made.) Why do you think these are called Bow-Wow in a Blankie? (Lead children to conclude how this recipe got its name.)

Technology Take-off Point

To learn how hot dogs are made, the history of hot dogs, nutritional information, and a virtual tour of a hot dog factory, go to the National Hotdog and Sausage Council home page at the following address:
http://www.hot-dog.org

Bow-Wow in a Blankie Recipe

Bow-Wow in a Blankie

Ingredients

hot dogs, one for each child

ready-to-bake biscuits, one or more for each child

ketchup

Directions

Roll up a hot dog in one or more biscuits. Bake the biscuit-covered hot dogs in the toaster oven, at the temperature recommended on the biscuit package, until the biscuit is golden brown. Let the Bow-Wow in a Blankie cool. Dip the Bow-Wow in ketchup and eat.

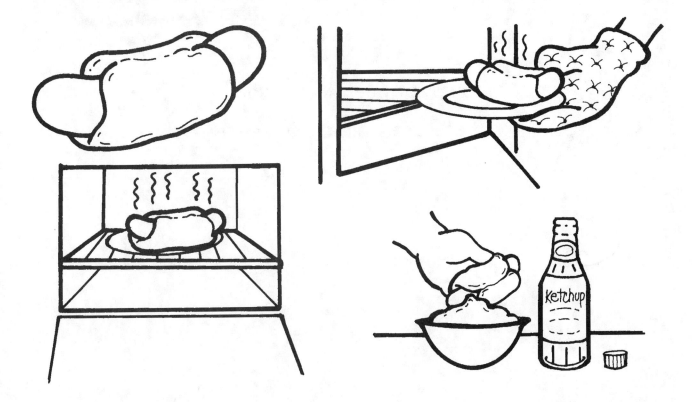

A Visit to the Zoo

Have you been to the zoo?
There are animals to see.
Have you been to the zoo?
Come on along with me!

A Visit to the Zoo (cont.)

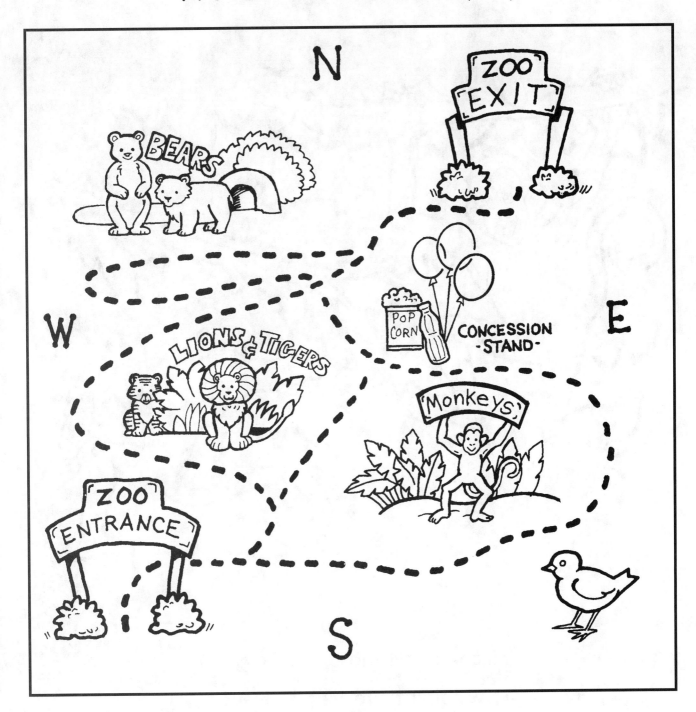

Let's all get a ticket,
And go in through the gate.
Let's look at the zoo map.
What fun! I just can't wait!

A Visit to the Zoo *(cont.)*

Look at all those monkeys
Swinging from tree to tree.
I think they look funny.
What do they think of me?

A Visit to the Zoo (cont.)

What has a long, long trunk,
Big ears, and little eyes?
Is it something scary?
No, elephants are nice.

A Visit to the Zoo (cont.)

Koala bears eat leaves
That grow on special trees.
Their fur is so fluffy,
You can't see their knees!

86

A Visit to the Zoo *(cont.)*

Mr. Owl sleeps all day long
So he can hunt at night.
When you hear him hoot,
Does it give you a fright?

A Visit to the Zoo (cont.)

Look at that big lion.
He looks so soft and sweet.
But don't touch a lion—
Your finger looks like meat!

88

A Visit to the Zoo *(cont.)*

The petting zoo is fun.
The animals are kind.
You can pet and love them.
And none of them will mind.

A Visit to the Zoo (cont.)

Now you've been to the zoo.
There's still a lot to see.
I'll come again someday.
Will you come back with me?

Around My House

Hands-On Internet Activities

Digital Pictures

This Is My Voice

Thematic Activities

Science—Machines in My Home

Storybook—My Web Site About Me

Annotated Web Sites

Parents Place

www.parentsplace.com

This site is aimed at providing parent education and suggesting ways to help you get parents interested in using the Internet at home with their children.

Library Spot

http://libraryspot.com/

Libraries are an important part of every child's community. This site has links to hundreds of home pages hosted by libraries. If you are planning to take children to the school or a local library or if you are just going to talk about libraries, visit this site first. Children can take virtual tours of typical libraries. Many online reference resources are available here.

Mr. Rogers' Neighborhood Home Page

http://www.pbs.org/rogers/

Children will be drawn to this friendly, fun Web site. There is a video message from Mr. Rogers welcoming students. Children can do a variety of activities, including take a tour of Mr. Rogers' home, listen to familiar songs, and journey to the Neighborhood of Make-Believe.

Better Homes and Gardens Learning Live Home Page

http://www.bhglive.com/education/preschool/index.html

Here is a site that has many interesting activities for preschoolers, as well as information about developmentally appropriate expectations for parents of preschoolers. Choose from activity pages that are appropriate for children from ages 2–3 or 3–4.

Grandparenting

http://www.parenting-qa.com/cgi-bin/detail/grandparenting/

Many grandparents are very involved in their grandchildren's lives. In some cases, grandparents are the children's primary caregivers or guardians. Share this Web site with grandparents.

Suggested Keyword Searches

machines, inventions, library, parents, grandparents, preschool activities, early childhood activities

Digital Pictures

Approximate Preparation Time

two hours

Learning Concept

This activity increases young children's computer literacy and improves their fine-motor coordination, computer mouse skills, self-esteem, and self-awareness.

Materials

- classroom computer
- Internet Service Provider
- digital camera or regular camera with film developed to CD-ROM
- Parent Permission for Internet Activities (page 16)

Warning: Be sure you have parent permission before sending anyone a child's photo as an e-mail attachment.

Lesson Preparation

Write a brief announcement about digital picture day and send it home to parents. Decide ahead of time if you would like children to dress up for pictures or just wear regular attire. Ask parents if they would like a digital picture of their child sent to them in an e-mail. Print a picture to send home to parents who do not have e-mail.

Circle and Center Time

Explain to children that you are going to take their pictures with a digital camera. Show children the camera and explain the major differences between regular cameras and digital cameras. Show children several regular photographs and then move to the computer so that they can compare a digital photo to a regular photo.

At the Computer

Take a digital picture of the whole class, and display it on the computer for children to see. If your camera has a display, show them the image first on the camera so they can compare it to the image they see on the computer screen. Repeat this process for individual pictures. Save each child's picture on a disk, labeling the disk with the child's name. Describe who is in the pictures. Model how to use the pronouns *me* and *I* so children will use them correctly when discussing their own pictures. E-mail the photos to parents who have given their permission.

What to Say

We are going to take class pictures today. First I'll take a picture of the whole class, and then I'll take one of each of you by yourself. These are special pictures that are taken with a camera called a digital camera. This type of camera works with the computer. (You may wish to have an adult helper take the picture of the entire class so you can be in it.)

This Is My Voice

Approximate Preparation Time

two hours

Learning Concept

Children have the opportunity to record and hear their own voices before sending a recorded message to their parents. This activity increases young children's computer literacy and improves their fine-motor coordination, self-esteem, and self-awareness.

Materials

- classroom computer with microphone
- Internet Service Provider (ISP)
- e-mail account
- computer microphone
- sound recorder for Windows or SimpleSound for Macintosh
- Parent Permission for Internet Activities (page 16)

Warning: Be sure you have parent permission before sending anyone a child's voice as an e-mail attachment.

Lesson Preparation

For this activity you must have a sound recorder software like the one that comes in the accessories package of Windows 95 or better for PCs or SimpleSound for MACs and a microphone. Practice until you are comfortable with the sound recorder before beginning this activity with children. You may wish to record an example for children to listen to. Write each child's name on a disk, so you can save the recording. As an alternative, make folders on the desktop with each child's name on a folder.

For parents who do not have e-mail, you may wish to invite them to stop by before, after, or during school so their children can share their recordings.

Note: Sometimes MAC sound files will not play on PC sound players. If you find that this is the case, save the recordings to disk so they can be played for parents at conferences or at an open house. Another option is to download a freeware (free software program) version of the MAC software called SoundApp. This program will allow MAC users to play sound files normally only available on PCs. Go to Macdownload.com at:

http://hotfiles.zdnet.com/cgi-bin/texis/swlib/hotfiles/info.html?fcode=MC10482&b=mac

In addition, if you will be sending e-mail to many parents with PCs, you may want to purchase Virtual PC, a software program that allows you to run Windows on your MAC.

This Is My Voice *(cont.)*

Circle Time

Explain the idea of making a voice e-mail for parents. Then talk with children about what they would like to say. Consider these examples:

- "Hi, Mommy. This is Gary. I love you!"
- "Happy birthday, Daddy! I made you a card today."
- "Hi, Mom. I am having a lot of fun at school today."
- Have the child recite a simple poem.

These are just suggestions to get you started. Children inevitably say sweet and adorable things that their parents treasure forever. After a few tries, most children get used to this kind of communication.

At the Computer

Follow the procedure detailed below for recording children's messages.

1. Plug in your computer microphone and hold it near the child or position the child near the built-in microphone on your computer.
2. Click Start. Drag to Programs, Accessories, Entertainment or Multimedia, and Sound Recorder. For Mac, click on the Apple and select SimpleSound. A menu bar will pop up.
3. Click on the *Record* button on the Sound Recorder dialog box as you ask a child to say a message for his or her parent. For a MAC, click on Speech Quality, drag to File, then New.
4 Remember to let children hear their own messages after they have finished recording. Allow them to rerecord their messages if they aren't happy with the original recordings.
5. After a child has finished the message, select File, Save As. The Save As dialog box will appear.
6. Save the file to a disk or desktop folder, and name the file so you can easily find it again.
7. Send the sound file as an e-mail attachment to the child's parent.
8. Decide on a friendly opening for the e-mail, such as, "Greetings from Garden Hill Preschool! Here is a voice message from your son Juan."

What to Say

Today we are going to send our mommies and daddies a special e-mail. We are going to record our voices and send our parents a message that is just for them.

Machines in My Home

Approximate Preparation Time

one hour

Learning Concept

This activity gives children an opportunity to explore science by guessing the functions of machines and then learning what the machines do. In addition, it enhances imagination and science literacy and improves vocabulary skills and cause-and-effect relationships.

Materials

*   various machines in your classroom
*   Machines in my Home checklist (page 96), one for each child

Warning: All machine demonstrations done in class or at home must be performed by adults or with adult supervision.

Lesson Preparation

Make a list of some machines in your classroom that you would like to point out to the children. Reproduce Machines at Home (page 96) for children.

Note: If you think parents will feel uncomfortable having their children tell what kinds of machines they have at home, restrict this activity to classroom or school machines.

Directed Teaching Focus

Discuss machines that are commonly seen in classrooms and homes. Ask children to name as many classroom machines as they can. Describe several classroom machines, telling what the machines do and demonstrating how they operate. Next, log on to the Internet to show children some pictures of machines that they might have in their homes.

Self-Directed Activity

Ask children to draw pictures of machines in the classroom or machines they have at home. Use blocks and other building materials for children to create their own "machines."

What to Say

Today we are going to learn more about the world around us. Who can tell me what a machine is? (Lead students to conclude that machines make work easier for people.) Let's take a look at some machines in our classroom and discover how we work them. (Point out the machines and show how to operate them.) Now we are going to look at some Web sites with photographs of machines. This will help you think of machines that you might have at home.

Technology Take-Off Point

Photographs of most machines available for home use are found on this easy-to-use Web site:
http://www.sears.com

Machines in My Home Checklist

We are learning about machines used at home. Help your child look at the machines in your home. Show your youngster how to work some of these machines. Check off the machines you demonstrate for your child.

- ❏ alarm clock
- ❏ blender
- ❏ CD player
- ❏ ceiling fan
- ❏ coffee maker
- ❏ computer
- ❏ dishwasher
- ❏ electric can opener
- ❏ electric hair curlers
- ❏ electric hair dryer
- ❏ electric mixer
- ❏ electric razor
- ❏ electric toothbrush
- ❏ garbage disposal
- ❏ gas fireplace
- ❏ kitchen timer
- ❏ lamps
- ❏ microwave oven
- ❏ oven
- ❏ popcorn popper
- ❏ radio
- ❏ refrigerator
- ❏ stereo
- ❏ stove
- ❏ television
- ❏ toaster or toaster oven
- ❏ VCR
- ❏ video game
- ❏ other: _____

My Web Site About Me

Hello. My name is _____.

This is my make-believe Web site.

My Web Site About Me *(cont.)*

This picture shows how I looked when I was a baby. I was much smaller back then!

My Web Site About Me *(cont.)*

I am _____ years old.

I have _____ hair and _____ eyes.

This picture shows what I look like now.

My Web Site About Me *(cont.)*

This picture shows my family.

The names of the people in my family are

_____

_____.

I love them very much, and they love me.

My Web Site About Me *(cont.)*

This picture shows where I live.

My Web Site About Me (cont.)

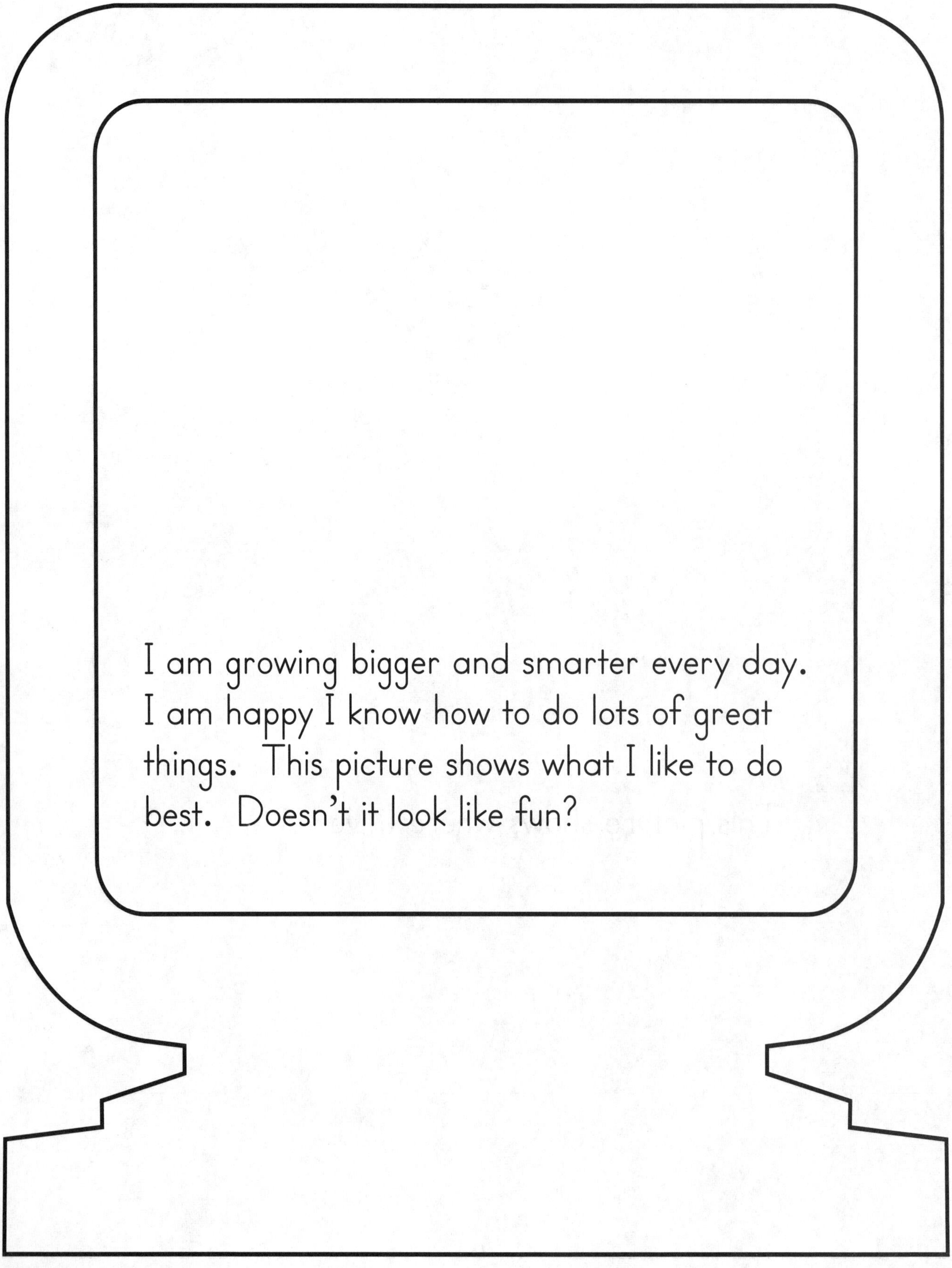

I am growing bigger and smarter every day. I am happy I know how to do lots of great things. This picture shows what I like to do best. Doesn't it look like fun?

Special People in History

Hands-On Internet Activities

Let's Go to the President's House

Some Special People in Early American History

Thematic Activities

Science—Recycled Sculpture Inventions

Cooking—Thanksgiving Cornucopia

Storybook—The First Thanksgiving

Annotated Web Sites

An American Thanksgiving

http://www.night.net/thanksgiving/

This site opens by playing the song "We Gather Together." Visit the Thanksgiving Fun link for games and more.

Historic Mount Vernon

http://www.mountvernon.org/

Take children on a virtual tour of Mount Vernon, George Washington's home. This site has a wealth of resources and is an excellent way to help introduce children to George Washington.

The Life of Abraham Lincoln

http://www.berwickacademy.org/lincoln/lincoln.htm

If you have ever wondered if a Web page would be a good idea for your classroom, this may help convince you. This page was constructed by a first grade class. It provides interesting information about Abraham Lincoln.

Betsy Ross Home Page

http://www.ushistory.org/betsy/flaghome.html

Preschoolers are just learning about the American flag and the Pledge of Allegiance. The Betsy Ross home page has lots of interesting information about our first flag, including a virtual tour of Betsy Ross' home. You can order a flag online if you wish.

Thanksgiving Mazes

http://www.kidsdomain.com/holiday/thanks/maze.html

These mazes are designed for children of various ages and have a Thanksgiving theme. The easiest mazes and those most appropriate for preschoolers are at the beginning of the list.

Suggested Keyword Searches

inventors, scientists, famous people, Pilgrims, Native Americans, Thanksgiving (You may also wish to search for the names of specific famous people.)

Let's Go to the President's House

Approximate Preparation Time

one hour

Learning Concept

This activity enhances young children's computer literacy, beginning social studies skills, fine-motor coordination, and verbal and reading readiness skills.

Materials

- classroom computer
- Internet Service Provider (ISP)
- bookmarked White House Web site: **www.whitehouse.gov/wh/kids/html/home.html**

Lesson Preparation

Go to the kids' section of the Official White House Web site ahead of time and carefully read over the material. Become familiar with the letter writing function of the site. Be sure to bookmark this site.

Circle Time

Before beginning this activity, introduce children to who the President of the United States is, what his job is, and where he lives. You may wish to check out children's library books on the subject and read them aloud, and then discuss what children know about the presidency. Bring in a newspaper or magazine picture of the current President and First Lady or print a picture from the White House Web site. Tell children that they will visit the White House and the First Family on the Internet and that they will be able to send an e-mail message to the President.

At the Computer

Take children to the White House Web site. Allow them to take a tour of the White House, and show them pictures the First Family. Talk with children about what they may want to ask the President, and help them compose an e-mail message. Print the e-mail message to display in your classroom. You may wish to enlarge the message on a copier before displaying it.

What to Say

We have been talking for the past few days about the person who is the leader of our country. What is that person called? (Lead children to conclude that the leader of our country is the President.) So far only men have been elected President, but a woman could also become President. Who is our President now? (Help children remember the name of the current President.) Where do the President and his family live? (Lead children to conclude that the President and his family live in the White House.) Today we will use the Internet to see the President's home. We will also see pictures of the President and the First Family. At the end of our visit, we will send the President an e-mail message.

Some Special People in Early American History

Approximate Preparation Time

two hours

Learning Concept

This activity supports young children's computer literacy, fine-motor coordination, and beginning social studies skills.

Materials

- classroom computer
- Internet Service Provider (ISP)
- bookmarked Web sites (page 103)
- Reader's Theater (pages 109 and 110), one copy for each child
- The First Thanksgiving (page 111), one copy for each child and one copy for presentation

Lesson Preparation

Preview and bookmark Web sites that you intend to use with students. Find at least one site for Native Americans and one for Pilgrims.

Reproduce the Reader's Theater so you can use it in conjunction with this activity. Create an invitation to send to parents and other guests if you would like children to present the Reader's Theater in front of an audience. You may wish to have parent volunteers provide refreshments for this event.

You can extend this lesson by having children make a Thanksgiving Cornucopia (pages 106–108).

At the Computer

Talk about who and what children will be seeing and learning about. Completing this research phase before reading the Reader's Theater will ensure that young children have a greater understanding of who the first settlers and native peoples were.

Circle and Center Time

Read aloud the Reader's Theater and show the picture of The First Thanksgiving (page 111). Tell children that they will be acting out parts in the story and that they will present the play to their parents and other guests. Then explain to children that they will use the Internet to learn more about Native Americans and the Pilgrims.

What to Say

We are going to learn more about the people we read about in our history story today. Let's visit a Web site that helps us learn more about _____. (Native Americans or Pilgrims)

Thanksgiving Cornucopia

Approximate Preparation Time

30 minutes

Learning Concept

Children have a food experience that does not require cooking. They make and fill their own Thanksgiving cornucopias. This activity enhances social studies literacy, creativity, and the ability to follow directions.

Materials

- materials and directions for Making a Thanksgiving Cornucopia (page 107)
- Cornucopia Pattern (page 108), one for each child

Warning: Ask parents if their children have any food allergies or dietary restrictions.

Lesson Preparation

Set up a Cooking Center with the directions and materials for making cornucopias. Arrange children's seating so that the lesson can be presented to the whole class or small groups. You may wish to enlist the help of volunteers. Remember to reproduce the recipe for the class cookbook and for student cookbooks that will be sent home at the end of the year. Reproduce the cornucopia pattern onto construction paper. You may wish to make the cornucopias ahead of time and simply have children decorate and fill them. To make each pattern, cut it out and cut the slit for the tab. Allow children to decorate the one side of the pattern. Then fit the tab through the slit, and secure the cone with tape.

Directed Teaching Focus

Introduce this activity by reading books about Thanksgiving and presenting information about this holiday using information from the Internet. (See the Technology Take-Off Point provided below.)

Self-Directed Activity

Have children make and decorate the cornucopia. Have them place the cornucopia on a paper plate and fill it with dried fruit, fresh fruit, and chocolate candies.

What to Say

We have been learning about how the Pilgrims and Native Americans celebrated the first Thanksgiving. Today you will be making a cornucopia, which is sometimes called a "horn of plenty." You will fill your cornucopia with good things to eat.

Technology Take-Off Point

The following Web site has plenty of ideas to help teach young children about Thanksgiving:
http://www.night.net/thanksgiving/

Making a Thanksgiving Cornucopia

Materials

raisins and other dried fruit

small apples and oranges

chocolate candies

Cornucopia Pattern (page 108), one for each child

construction paper

glue

scissors

tape

glitter

crayons

paper plate

Directions

Cut out the pattern. Cut the slit for the tab. Use crayons to color the cornucopia and/or decorate it with pieces of construction paper and glitter. Then fit the tab through the slit, and secure the cone with tape. Place the finished cornucopia on a paper plate. Fill the cornucopia with good things to eat. You may wish to use your cornucopia as the centerpiece for your dinner table on Thanksgiving.

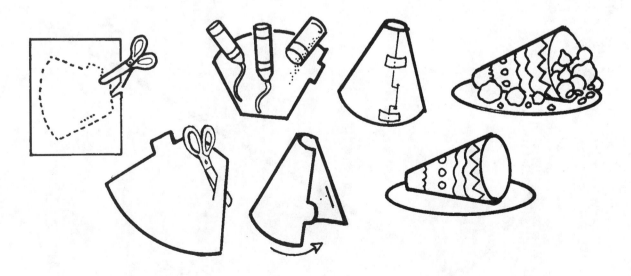

Cornucopia Pattern

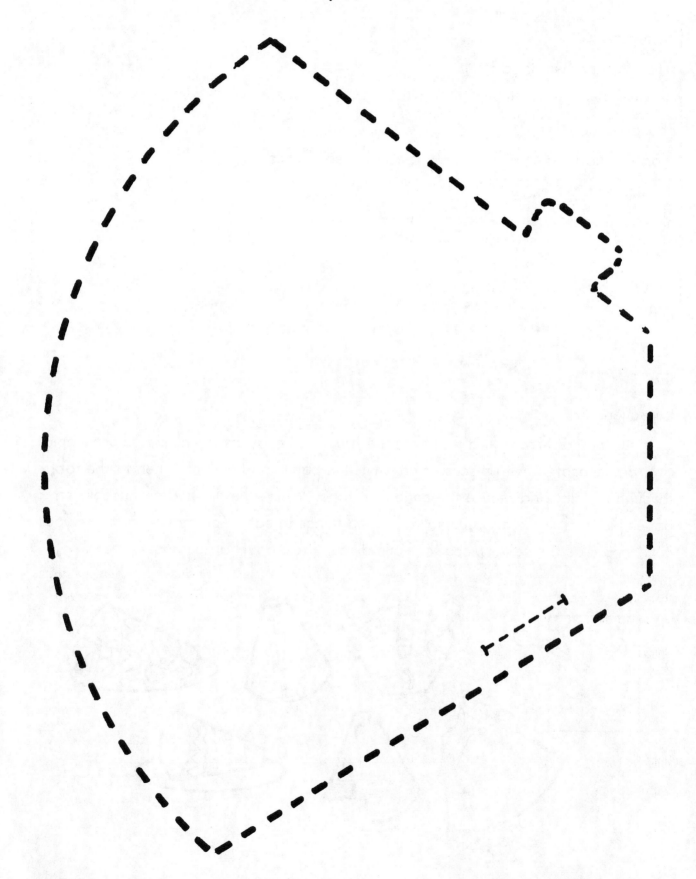

The First Thanksgiving Reader's Theater

Note to Parents:

When you read this reader's theater with your child, ask your child to help you read the children's parts. Do this by pointing to the line, and saying, "You say…." Point to each word as you say the line. Ask your child to repeat the words after you say them. Your child might want to point to the words while reading them. By reading this together, you are improving your child's reading readiness skills, such as tracking and word recognition.

If your child is presenting this reader's theater to an audience at school, your youngster will need your help to memorize one or two lines. Use the same activity described above, but concentrate on the line(s) your child needs to memorize. Repeat the activity frequently before the day of the presentation so your child feels comfortable saying the line(s).

Note to Teacher: For this reader's theater, you may wish to make simple, paper costumes for the Native Americans and the Pilgrims. Use pictures of food or plastic or real food for props. Depending on the number of students in your class, you may need to have a couple of children say each line or assign more than one line to each child.

The First Thanksgiving

Child 1: Welcome to our reader's theater, which will tell the story of the first Thanksgiving.

Narrator: Long ago, before the United States was a country, people lived in the land called America. The very first people in America were called Native Americans.

Child 2: (*dressed as a Native American*) I am a Native American.

Narrator: For many years, the Native Americans lived on the land we now call America. Then one day other people came to this land. These people were called Pilgrims. They traveled across the ocean on a ship called the *Mayflower*.

Child 3: (*dressed as a Pilgrim*) I am a Pilgrim.

Narrator: The pilgrims came to America because they wanted to be able to practice their religion the way they thought was right. Their ship landed at a place called Plymouth Rock. They suffered many hardships when they got to America.

Child 4: (*dressed as a Pilgrim*) The winter is very cold here.

Child 5: (*dressed as a Pilgrim*) We don't have enough food.

Child 6: (*dressed as a Pilgrim*) What will we do?

The First Thanksgiving
Reader's Theater *(cont.)*

Narrator: The Pilgrims and the Native Americans became friends.

Child 7: *(dressed as a Pilgrim)* We are friends with the Native Americans. Maybe they can help us.

(Have the Pilgrims and the Native Americans join hands, then let go.)

Child 8: *(dressed as a Native American)* I am a Native American. I helped the Pilgrims plant their corn. *(show ear of corn)*

Child 9: *(dressed as a Pilgrim)* Thank you, Native Americans, for helping us.

Narrator: To celebrate the harvest, the Pilgrims and Native Americans got together and had a big feast that is now called the first Thanksgiving.

Child 10: *(dressed as a Native American or a Pilgrim)* I am bringing apples to the Thanksgiving feast. *(show some apples)*

Child 11: *(dressed as a Native American or a Pilgrim)* I am bringing a turkey to the Thanksgiving feast. *(show a turkey)*

Child 12: *(dressed as a Native American or a Pilgrim)* I am bringing nuts to the Thanksgiving feast. *(show some nuts)*

Child 13: *(dressed as a Native American or a Pilgrim)* I am bringing cranberries to the Thanksgiving feast. *(show some cranberries)*

Child 14: *(dressed as a Native American or a Pilgrim)* I am bringing corn to the Thanksgiving feast. *(show some corn)*

Child 15: *(dressed as a Native American or a Pilgrim)* I am bringing a pumpkin to the Thanksgiving feast. *(show a pumpkin)*

(Be sure some children are dressed as Pilgrims and others as Native Americans. You can add more foods, depending upon the number of children participating.)

Narrator: The first Thanksgiving was a wonderful party. The Pilgrims and the Native Americans were thankful for their food. Today many people in America celebrate Thanksgiving. We are still thankful for the good things we have to eat.

Children: We are thankful for our food. Happy Thanksgiving!

The First Thanksgiving

Fascinating Food

Hands-On Internet Activities

Virtual Food

Virtual Field Trip

Thematic Activities

Cooking—Inventor's Sundaes

Mathematics—Cooking Math

Storybook—The Land of Yummy

Annotated Web Sites

FDA Kids Home page

http://www.fda.gov/oc/opacom/kids/

This is an excellent site for basic information about the Food and Drug Administration (FDA). There is a coloring book that that teaches young children about nutritious eating habits and health.

Benny Goodsport and the Good Sport Gang

http://www.bennygoodsport.com/

Benny Goodsport and his friends teach children about fitness and the food pyramid. Just as you would present a picture book, read this site to children as you show them the illustrations.

Food Fun for Kids

http://www.nppc.org/foodfun.html

This site was created by the National Pork Board and offers children fun activities and nutrition information. One wonderful part of this site is their "Farmtastic" Voyage in which children visit baby pigs on a farm. For teachers and parents, there are recipes and informative links.

Chocolate World

http://www.hersheys.com/chocworld/

The makers of Hershey's chocolate present coloring activities, music for children, information about chocolate, and much more. This is an excellent site to search for the different food activities in this unit.

Suggested Keyword Searches

food, food pyramid, nutrition, fitness, healthy habits, health, dairy, virtual tours (You may also wish to search for the names of specific foods.)

Virtual Food

Approximate Preparation Time
two hours

Learning Concept
This activity enhances computer literacy skills and improves fine-motor skills.

Materials
- classroom computer
- printer
- 3.5-inch floppy disks, one for each child (optional)

- Internet Service Provider (ISP)
- printer paper

Lesson Preparation
Preview and bookmark Web sites that show the foods you listed during Circle Time. Label a disk with each child's name or make folders on the hard drive labeled with children's names.

Circle Time
Start this activity at Circle Time and chat with children about their favorite foods. Make a list of these. Consider asking for two different favorites from each child in case you have trouble finding Internet pictures of a certain food. Then tell children that they will get a chance to look at a picture of their favorite foods and save it on the computer.

At the Computer
Use the following steps and page 304 to help children save their food pictures.

1. On a PC, right click on the picture of the food. Click on Save Picture As. For a Mac, click and hold until the floating menu appears. Then click, "Save this image as . . . ."

2. In the Save Picture dialog box that appears, type your file name. You might wish to use the name of the food or a shortened form of it and the child's initials as the file name. On a PC, make sure to save the picture to your A drive if you are saving on individual disks. Otherwise save to the folders on your C drive (hard drive). For a Mac, save to folders on the desktop for easy access, or save to disk by double clicking on the desktop icon, locating the image icon file, and double clicking again.

3. Click Save.

4. Show children how to open the file. On a PC, have them view it in Windows by clicking Start and Run and then typing "A:\." Next, have them click OK and then double-click on the correct file icon. For a Mac, double-click the file icon on your desktop.

What to Say
Today I am going to write down everyone's favorite food. Then later this week you will look at a picture of your favorite food on the Internet and save it on the computer. (Lead children through the process of locating their picture on the bookmarked Web sites, opening it, and saving it in a folder on the hard drive or on a disk.)

Virtual Field Trip

Approximate Preparation Time
one hour

Learning Concept

This activity introduces young children the concept of
virtual tours. Like an armchair traveler, the Internet
provides children the opportunity to visit and explore
many places that they might not be able to visit in real
life. This activity increases young children's computer
literacy, and fine-motor, reading readiness, and
vocabulary skills.

Materials

- classroom computer
- Internet Service Provider (ISP)
- bookmarked dairy Web site: **http://www.moomilk.com**
- bookmarked Web sites with virtual tours
- The Land of Yummy storybook (pages 118–125)

Lesson Preparation

This activity is based on "Moo Milk—A Dynamic Adventure into the Dairy Industry" however you can
use any virtual tour site. Search for food industry Web sites and large food corporations for potential
virtual tours. Be sure to preview and bookmark any Web sites that you intend to use with students.

Circle and Center Time

Introduce this activity using the big book version of The Land of Yummy storybook. Then you may
wish to discuss the different types of food groups on the food pyramid and what dairy products are.
Tell children that they are going on an Internet field trip, called a "virtual tour," to a dairy.

At the Computer

Access the Web site and remind children that they are going on a virtual tour of a real dairy. Let
children click from one link on the tour to the next. Give children plenty of time to look at the pictures
and make sure to read aloud any relevant text.

What to Say

We are going on a field trip using our computer. This type of field trip is called a "virtual tour." Using
the Internet, the computer will take us to see a real dairy with real dairy cows. On our tour, we will get
to see how people get milk from cows. (Enlist the help of children to click the mouse as your class
moves from one part of the virtual tour to the next.)

Inventor's Sundaes

Approximate Preparation Time

30 minutes

Learning Concept

This activity enhances children's creativity, decision-making skills, and fine-motor coordination.

Materials

- ingredients and recipe for Inventor's Sundae (page 116)
- plastic, Styrofoam, or paper bowls
- plastic spoons
- large serving spoon or ice cream scoop
- napkins

Warning: Ask parents if their children have any food allergies or dietary restrictions.

Lesson Preparation

After students brainstorm a list of sundae toppings, purchase a variety of these. Then set up a Cooking Center with the recipe and ingredients for making sundaes. Arrange children's seating so that the lesson can be presented to the whole class or small groups. Remember to reproduce the recipe for the class cookbook and for student cookbooks that will be sent home at the end of the year.

Directed Teaching Focus

Ahead of time, have children brainstorm a list of toppings that they would like to put on an ice cream sundae. Write these on the board. After purchasing the sundae ingredients, tell children which toppings they may choose from when creating their sundaes. Place the materials and ingredients in the Cooking Center. Model how to make a sundae. Then allow children to make their sundaes, choosing any toppings they like.

Self-Directed Activity

Invite children to color the picture of the sundae on the recipe.

What to Say

We have been learning interesting things about food, and I think it will be fun for you to invent your own ice-cream sundae recipe. First, I need to know what kinds of toppings you would like on your sundaes. (Write the list on the board. Set a date for the sundae-making activity.) (After the Cooking Center is set up with all the necessary materials and ingredients, continue.) Let me show you how to make a sundae. Remember, when it is your turn, you will get to make up your own special recipe so be sure to choose the toppings that you like.

Technology Take-Off Point

Ice cream is so much fun, you will probably want to indulge some more. This is easy to do at Ben and Jerry's official Web site located at:

http://euphoria.benjerry.com/

Recipe for Inventor's Sundaes

Inventor's Sundae

Ingredients

ice cream

toppings such as:

candy	miniature marshmallows
fruit	whipped cream
o-shaped cereal	chocolate syrup
alphabet cereal	butterscotch syrup

Directions

Put a scoop of ice cream in a bowl. Add the toppings of your choice.

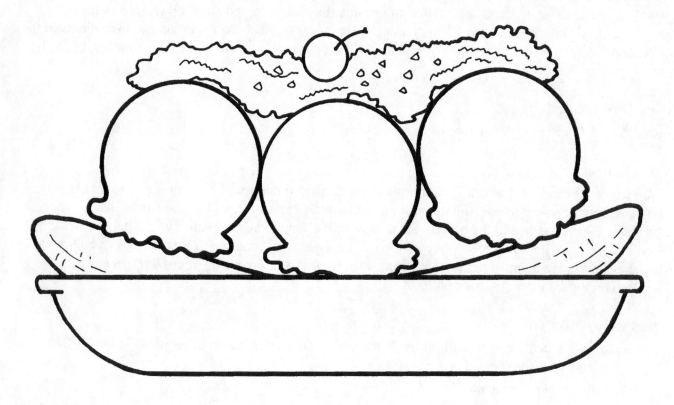

Cooking Math

Approximate Preparation Time

30 minutes

Learning Concept

This activity teaches basic measurement skills and improves fine-motor coordination and understanding of spatial relations.

Materials

- rice
- water
- measuring cups
- large workspace
- large bowls

- flour
- measuring spoons
- blunt plastic knives or plastic ruler
- drop cloth

Lesson Preparation

Prepare for this activity by creating a Cooking/Math Center. Put a drop cloth on the floor before beginning to cut down on clean up time. Decide ahead of time if you want to do just a liquids or solids measurement activity or one of each on different days.

Directed Teaching Focus

- **Liquids**—Give each child a large bowl filled with water into which he/she can dip measuring spoons and measuring cups. Have different-sized containers for children to estimate how many units, such as tablespoons and cups, will be needed to fill the containers with water.
- **Solids**—Give each child a blunt plastic knife or a plastic ruler. Show them how to level the solid ingredients. Give children large bowls to pour their measured ingredients. Consider just one type of solid ingredient at a time to prevent children from combining them.

Self-Directed Activity

Set up a water table and include the measuring spoons and measuring cups for children to use in self-directed play.

What to Say

Today we have a center with measuring spoons and measuring cups. We will start by measuring (liquids or solids). (Explain what liquids and solids are as you present each type of lesson.) (Model how to measure liquids and dry ingredients.)

Technology Take-Off Point

Food for Tots, located at the Web site shown below, has fun and interesting nutrition information for preschoolers. You can request an informative nutrition newsletter, find recipes, ask specific nutrition questions, print coloring pages, and show children flash videos.

http://www.foodfortots.com/

The Land of Yummy

I have a special place I go
Whenever I go to sleep.
My dreamtime land's so tasty,
I go to bed without a peep.

This special place I love to go
Is happy for my tummy.
I think you may not be surprised,
It's the dreamtime Land of Yummy!

The Land of Yummy *(cont.)*

I take a dip in the Apple Juice Sea,

And toss around a pumpkin ball.

And after that, if I'm not tired,

I dance around Cupcake Hall.

And when my legs are tired,

With sore and aching feet,

I skip to the Yummy Land Restaurant,

And get myself a treat.

The Land of Yummy (cont.)

I sit at a little table
With a napkin on my lap,
And order from the menu--
A little of this and that.

And when the server brings it
Hot and steamy on a tray,
It looks so good, I just can't wait.
Oh, yes! It's a yummy day.

The Land of Yummy (cont.)

I choose from the food pyramid,
With lots of things from the bottom.
I'd like some lovely spaghetti,
Potatoes and rice if you've got them.

I make sure I eat vegetables.
I really love the taste.
And then I have some dairy,
Meat, or fish upon my plate.

The Land of Yummy (cont.)

I eat just until I am full,
So I have a comfortable tummy.
And then I save a little room,
For a nibble of something yummy.

I have a taste of pie or cake,
Or perhaps a chocolate or two.
And then I leave the restaurant,
There's so much to see and do.

The Land of Yummy *(cont.)*

I help the Yummy Land farmer
As she tends to her vegetable crops.
I put up all the food that's ripe
In a basket so nothing drops.

I help her with the planting
Of little seedlings in the ground.
And when we're done, I sprinkle water
Gently all around.

The Land of Yummy (cont.)

I go to the Yummy Land bakery,
And watch the baker bake bread.
I sniff and sniff the yummy air,
And can almost taste it instead.

The baker gives me a cookie
Shaped like a happy face.
I really love my Yummy Land,
It's such a happy place.

The Land of Yummy (cont.)

And now its time to go away.
The sun's about to rise.
I say goodbye and hurry home,
And rub the sleep out of my eyes.

My mom's about to make breakfast,
And I don't want to be rude.
I don't think I can eat a bite,
I'm so stuffed with make-believe food.

Friends Around the World

Hands-On Internet Activities

Global Exploration

Friends Around the World

Thematic Activities

Cooking—Burritos Buenos

Art—Ikebana: Japanese Floral Arrangement

Storybook—My Mom's Salad Bowl

Annotated Web Sites

Hello in Many Languages

http://www.elite.net/~runner/jennifers/hello.htm

This is an interesting place for you to start your research on multiculturalism and its various themes. You may wish to teach your children a new way of saying "hello" each week.

Hanukkah Activities for Preschool Children

http://www.perpetualpreschool.com/hanukkah.htm

Learn some wonderful activities for preschoolers to celebrate Hanukkah and other Jewish holidays at this site by the Perpetual Preschool.

Connecting Kids Around the World

http://www.kidsdomain.com/review/features/kidsaroundworld.html

While you are looking for ways to make young children become aware of other kinds of people and other cultures, make sure you don't miss this vast supply of interesting links, all with one thing in common: using the Internet as a global connection for kids. Consider this site as a starting point in your search for global pen pals and communication.

Global Show-n-Tell

http://www.telenaut.com/gst/

Here is an online art gallery for kids to exhibit their work from around the world. The site gives information for teachers and parents about how to enter children's work.

UNICEF Voices of Youth Home page

http://www.unicef.org/voy/

This site is NOT appropriate for children, but it may be useful to you for information about anti-bias and global issues. There is a teacher forum here for you to share your ideas. The text is available in English, Spanish, and French.

Suggested Keyword Searches

holidays, celebrations, festivals, children's art work, multicultural, traditions, international recipes (You may also wish to search for the names of specific cultures or ethnicities.)

Global Exploration

Approximate Preparation Time

one hour

Learning Concept

This activity teaches young children computer literacy and beginning map skills, and improves their fine-motor coordination, memory skills, and their understanding of the world around them.

Materials

- classroom computer
- Internet Service Provider (ISP)
- bookmarked Web sites (page 126)
- computer printer
- printer paper
- world globe

Lesson Preparation

Preview and bookmark Web sites that you intend to use with students. Pick places that you want children to see, or allow children to pick the locations.

Note: If you plan to allow children to pick the places, the best way to do this in an early childhood setting is to let one child pick a place each day or week.

Circle and Center Time

Show children the globe. Explain what it is. Talk about where your community is located on the globe. If children have any friends or family in other places that they can name, find those places and point them out.

At the Computer

Move to the computer and explore the bookmarked sites. In places where you deem it appropriate, let children point and click the mouse. Give each child a chance to operate the mouse.

What to Say

Today we are going to use the Internet to visit _____. (Name the place.) Let me show you where _____ is on the globe. (Name the place and point to its location on the globe.) This is where we live. (Point to the general location of your community on the globe.) We will have to use our computer to travel all the way from here to _____. (Name the place you are going to look at on the Internet, and use your finger to show the route from your community to that place on the globe.)

Friends Around the World

Approximate Preparation Time
one hour

Learning Concept
This activity increases children's understanding of multiculturalism and encourages tolerance, while enhancing oral language skills, computer literacy, fine-motor coordination, and sequencing skills.

Materials
- classroom computer
- Internet Service Provider (ISP)
- e-mail account
- Parent Permission Letter (page 129), one for each child

Lesson Preparation
Enlist the help of parents by sending home the letter on page 129. Assemble the contacts they have provided so you know a little bit about the person to whom the class will be writing and how they are related to someone in the class.

As you receive a response from parents that includes e-mail addresses of friends or relatives around the globe, send an introduction e-mail to confirm their willingness to participate. Then add their address to your address book.

Circle Time
After hearing back from parents, explain the activity to children. Talk about who they will send the letters to, and plan the letters together. Put little flags on a map to show where e-mail responses come from.

At the Computer
Write the letter to a specific e-mail recipient as children watch. Let them tell you what to write. Talk it over and then read what you wrote. Let a different child select the address from the address book and click the button to send the letter. Read responses to children as they are received. Encourage participants to send pictures or other downloads of interest for children. Always check the mail before presenting it to children, including any downloads or pictures.

What to Say
We have a new pen pal in England. This person is a preschool teacher in London, and she is Ginny's mom's sister. This is how we made this new friend. Shall we plan an e-mail for her? What shall we ask her? What do you want to say? Why don't we send her a class picture? Let's talk about it and then you can help me send the letter online.

Parent Permission Letter

_____

Date

Dear Parent(s),

As part of our unit called "Friends Around the World," we are trying to send and receive e-mail from as many different places around the globe as possible. We hope that you will be able to help us with this activity.

If you have friends or family members who have an e-mail address and who live in other towns, cities, states, provinces, or countries, please ask if they would like to participate in our Friends Around the Globe E-mail Project.

Our class would like to write and send short e-mails to these friends and family members. In return, our class would like to get an e-mail response from these people.

Please provide the following information about a friend or family member who would like to participate in this activity:

- full name of contact: _____
- relationship to you and your child: _____
- e-mail address: _____
- location: _____

If you know other people whom we may contact, please use the back of this letter to write the above information for each person.

If you have any questions, please feel free to give me a call. Thank you for helping to make this activity a valuable learning experience for your child.

Sincerely,

_____
Teacher

_____
School

_____
Phone

Burritos Buenos

Approximate Preparation Time
30 minutes

Learning Concept
Making these burritos enhances children's cultural awareness. Additionally, this activity improves children's fine-motor coordination and their ability to follow directions.

Materials

- world globe
- ingredients and recipe for Burritos Buenos (page 132)
- can opener
- paper plates
- blunt or plastic knives
- napkins
- microwave oven (optional)
- wooden or plastic toothpicks (optional)
- bookmarked Web sites that show foods from around the world

Warnings: Ask parents if their children have any food allergies or dietary restrictions. Never allow children near the microwave or to handle anything that is hot.

Lesson Preparation
Preview and bookmark Web sites that you intend to use with students.

Set up a Cooking Center with the recipe and ingredients for making burritos. Arrange children's seating so that the lesson can be presented to the whole class or small groups. You may wish to enlist the help of volunteers.

Remember to reproduce the recipe for the class cookbook and for student cookbooks that will be sent home at the end of the year.

Prepare for this activity by researching a few different but familiar foods that originate in different cultures. Consider some of these search ideas: search using the words *international recipes, cultural diversity,* or using the name of a country or region and the word *recipes* (i.e., *Asian recipes*).

You may wish to extend this lesson by presenting some examples of foods from various cultures. Consider the following ideas:

- Make or buy several examples and bring them to school for children to taste.
- Ask interested parents to make a traditional recipe from a culture of their choice to share with the class. Parents can also be invited to introduce the dish, tell which culture it is from, and describe how they made it.
- Show children Internet pictures of foods from different cultures.

Burritos Buenos *(cont.)*

You may wish to print a variety of Internet pictures showing foods from different cultures. Place them in a three-ring binder for your class library. Title the binder "Foods from Around the World." This kind of a picture book will be interesting for children to look at during self-directed center time.

Directed Teaching Focus

As you describe a food that you are showing your class (either the real food or a picture of the food), use the globe to point out where the food comes from. Even though young children won't be able to completely understand the concept of the various countries on a globe, this exercise will give them a beginning foundation for later learning in this area.

Move to the Cooking Center. Open the can(s) of refried beans. Model how to make a burrito. Use a dull knife to take the beans out of the can, and help each child spread some beans on a tortilla. Place the grated cheese in a bowl, and invite children to sprinkle cheese over the beans. (Make sure that they wash their hands first!) Show children how to roll the burrito. You may wish to use toothpicks to hold the tortillas in place. Then you or an adult helper can heat the burritos in the microwave. Cook the burritos one at a time for 30 seconds or less. Check to be sure they are not too hot before giving them to children.

Discuss the differences in foods and recipes from different cultures around the world. Talk about and show pictures of some common foods from a variety of cultures that children might already know. These pictures can be from numerous sources, including magazines, cookbooks, and the Internet.

Self-Directed Activity

If you have made a "Foods from Around the World" binder, allow children to look at it.

What to Say

People all over the world enjoy different kinds of food. If you went on a trip around the world and stopped in many places, you would have a chance to try foods that you have never eaten before. I will show you some foods and tell you where they came from. Then you can tell me if you have ever tried these foods. (Show pictures and ask children if they have eaten those foods.)

Today we are going to make a food called a burrito. It comes from Mexico. Has anyone here ever had a burrito before? (Allow children to respond.) Now I will show you how to make a burrito. Then you will make your own. (Model how to make a burrito. When children make their burritos, provide assistance as needed. Make sure that only an adult uses the microwave.)

Technology Take-Off Point

Try the following sites for some international recipes:

http://members.tripod.com/~GabyandAndy/Internation_Recipes.html

http://www.qvctc.commnet.edu/student/annekellner/recipes.html

Burritos Buenos Recipe

Burritos Buenos

Ingredients

flour tortillas

canned refried beans

grated cheese

paper plates

napkins

Directions

Spread beans on a flour tortilla. Sprinkle grated cheese over the beans. Roll the tortilla. You may wish to use a toothpick to hold the rolled tortilla in place. Place the burrito on a paper plate. Eat cold or have an adult warm the burrito in the microwave for 30 seconds. Make sure the burrito isn't too hot before you eat it.

Ikebana: Japanese Floral Arrangement

Approximate Preparation Time

one hour

Learning Concept

Ikebana—the Japanese art of floral arrangement—enhances children's cultural awareness by introducing them to an art form from another culture. It also supports children's creativity, listening skills, and fine-motor coordination.

Materials

- clean, empty plastic one-liter or one-quart bottles, one for each child
- spray paint (optional)

- cut or silk flowers (various types)
- thin sticks or branches
- bookmarked *ikebana* Web sites

Lesson Preparation

Preview and bookmark Web sites that you intend to use with students. Set up an Art Center with the necessary materials. You may want to spray paint the plastic bottles before placing them in the center. Buy a number of sturdy, reasonably priced cut flowers or silk flowers to put in the center. For real flowers, consider carnations or daisies since both last a long time and resist being damaged when handled by youngsters. Gather thin, interestingly shaped sticks in a park or the on the school grounds for the center. Children can help you with this task.

Directed Teaching Focus

Use the bookmarked Web sites to show children examples of *ikebana*. For a starting place, see the URL (Web site address) provided below in the Technology Take-Off Point. Model *ikebana* for children by creatively arranging the sticks and flowers in a bottle. Explain that the Japanese call this type of flower arrangement *ikebana*. Tell children that there are three parts, or elements, to the arrangement. The three parts represent the earth, the spirit, and people. Then have children make their own arrangements.

Self-Directed Activity

Allow children to arrange and rearrange the flowers and sticks. As an alternative, you may wish to have children draw pictures to show different arrangements rather than actually making them.

What to Say

Today we are going to learn about *ikebana*, which is a Japanese flower arrangement. (Invite children to say i-kA-'bä-nä with you.) You will need a plastic bottle for a vase and three things from nature—two sticks and a flower. You will use these to make a beautiful arrangement.

Technology Take-Off Point

The following Web site features a variety of excellent photographs and detailed information about *ikebana*:

http://www.asahi-net.or.jp/~tv9s-kbys/eindex.htm

My Mom's Salad Bowl

My mom says the world is like a salad bowl.

It is a big bowl full of different kinds of people.

My Mom's Salad Bowl (cont.)

My mom doesn't mean a real salad bowl.

She means the world is full of people from different cultures and with different customs.

My Mom's Salad Bowl (cont.)

My mom says the world is like a salad bowl.

She says it's like a big bowl of people who need to be nice to each other when they work and play together.

My Mom's Salad Bowl (cont.)

My mom doesn't mean a real salad bowl.

She means we need to be nice to each other no matter where we are. Like on the playground, we should take turns, share, and make sure we don't hurt others.

My Mom's Salad Bowl *(cont.)*

My mom says the world is like a salad bowl.

She says we are all different in some ways, but we care about many of the same things. We love our families. We want to have friends. We want to learn and have fun.

138

My Mom's Salad Bowl (cont.)

My mom says the world is like a salad bowl.

She means we all belong to the same world, and we must get along together.

Numbers

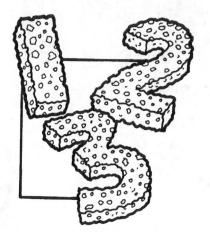

Hands-On Internet Activities

Taking Turns at the Computer

Matching Real Photos to Illustrations

Thematic Activities

Art—Sponge Numbers

Cooking—Bugs in a Rug

Counting Book—In the Garden

Annotated Web Sites

Learning Numbers Through Play Activities

http://www.topmarks.co.uk/parents/numbers.htm

Topmarks is an organization in England that has some interesting resources for early childhood teachers. This Learning Numbers page offers a number activities comprised of four skill areas.

Children's Television Playground Preschool Playground

http://www.ctw.org/preschool/0,1129,,00.html

This site makes it easy for you and your student to build your own Web site. Activities involving Sesame Street characters reinforce reading and math readiness and memory skills.

The Eisenhower National Clearinghouse for Mathematics and Science Education

http://www.enc.org/fr_index.htm

This is an amazing resource. Its search engine is the gateway to a wealth of knowledge in mathematics and science for prekindergarten classrooms.

Preschool Shareware and Freeware

http://shareware.about.com/library/bl9802e1.htm?iam=ask&terms=where+can+I+teach+my+toddler+about+shapes%3F

This excellent site researches and pulls together relevant information about freeware (free software) that you can use in your early childhood classroom. This site features information about free software programs that teach toddlers and preschoolers numbers, shapes, letters, letter-sound recognition, and more.

Suggested Keyword Searches

preschool, prekindergarten, readiness skills (You may also wish to search for specific skills that you are teaching the children.)

Taking Turns at the Computer

Approximate Preparation Time
one hour

Learning Concept
Children learn to recognize the numbers 1, 2, and 3 and how these numbers relate to sequencing things as first, second, and third.

Materials
- classroom computer
- Internet Service Provider (ISP)
- bookmarked Web sites (page 140)
- cardstock, three different colors
- scissors
- laminator and laminating film or clear Contact paper
- hole punch
- yarn
- black wide-tipped marker

Lesson Preparation
Preview and bookmark Web sites that you intend to use with students.

Make three "Take a Turn" badges. Start by cutting three identical circles out of different colors of cardstock. Use a black wide-tipped marker to number the badges 1, 2, and 3. Laminate the badges or use clear Contact paper to cover them. Then punch a hole at the top of each. String a piece of yarn through each hole and tie the ends in a knot. Be sure the pieces of yarn are long enough for children to slip them on and off over their heads.

Circle and Center Time
Introduce children to the numbers 1, 2, and 3. Talk about what it means to be first, second, and third. Invite children to provide example of times when people use ordinal numbers (first, second, third).

At the Computer
Put the badges face down. Let three children at a time choose a badge. Ask each child to tell you the number on the badge and then put it around his or her neck. Open a Web site and allow children with badges to select or do something in the order of the numbers on their badges.

What to Say
We are going take turns using the computer. _____ will be the first group to work on the computer. (Name three children. Have those children come up to the computer. Be sure the badges are face down in the Computer Center.) Each of you take one of these badges and turn it over. Can you tell me what your number is? (Help children who do not recognize the number on their badges.) Now I want you to put on your badges. The child wearing number 1 will have the first turn, number 2 will have the second turn, and number 3 will have the third turn. After these three have finished taking their turns, three more of you will get to take turns. We will continue learning how to take turns until everyone has come to work on the computer.

Matching Real Photos to Illustrations

Approximate Preparation Time

Several hours

Learning Concept

Children learn the mathematical concept of one-to-one correspondence. In addition, this activity improves young children's computer literacy, fine-motor coordination, and ability to sort and match information.

Materials

- classroom computer
- Internet Service Provider (ISP)
- bookmarked Web sites (page 140)
- computer printer

- printer paper
- table for children's insect exhibit
- In the Garden counting book (pages 146–155)

Lesson Preparation

Preview and bookmark Web sites that you intend to use with students. You may wish to use the search engine **Ask.com** to search for insect sites. Ask the question: *Where can I see photographs of insects?* Find and print a photograph of for each insect shown in the counting book In the Garden. Display the copies of the photographs and the drawings from the storybook on a table.

Circle Time

Read the big book version of In the Garden to children. Discuss with children how the pictures they see in the book are drawings that someone made, just like the pictures they make when they color or draw. Then show children the bug photographs that you printed from the Internet. Explain that the photograph was taken with a camera.

At the Computer

Open a bookmarked Web site. Allow children to view the photographs of the different insects. In places where you deem it appropriate, let children point and click the mouse.

What to Say

Now that we have read this interesting counting book about bugs, I thought it might be fun to find photographs of these bugs on the Internet. (Display the first page of the counting book and show children the picture of a grasshopper.) Look at the drawing of a grasshopper in our book. This is a drawing that an artist made for the book. It is just like the pictures you draw in our classroom Art Center. (Display a photograph of a grasshopper.) This picture is also of a grasshopper. However, it is different from the picture in our book. It is a photograph taken of a real bug that is made with a camera. (Display the grasshopper drawing and photograph.) Let's look at the drawing and the photograph at the same time. Then we can see how they are alike and how they are different. (Discuss the similarities and differences. Then continue this process with other bugs shown in the counting book.)

Sponge Numbers

Approximate Preparation Time

one hour

Learning Concept

Children enjoy an art experience that continues to familiarize them with counting from one to ten. This activity enhances number recognition and vocabulary, eye-hand coordination, and listening skills.

Materials

- ten new sponges
- poster paints, various colors
- shallow pans, one for each color paint
- paper towels
- brown paper lunch bags, one for each child
- ribbon (optional)
- paint smocks
- sharp scissors or utility knife, for adult use only

Lesson Preparation

Cut the sponges into the numbers: 1, 2, 3, 4, 5, 6, 7, 8, 9, 0. Pour each color paint into a separate shallow pan. Place the number sponges and bags at the center.

Directed Teaching Focus

Review the numbers 1–10. Model how to dip the sponges in paint and use them to stamp numbers on a brown paper bag. Remind children to let the paint dry on one side before decorating the other side. Show them that the number 10 can be made using the 1 and 0 sponges. Tell children that they may use the bags as wrapping paper for a present.

Self-Directed Activity

Children should be able to use the number sponges anytime you allow self-directed painting.

What to Say

We are going to have fun with numbers today. Look at these sponges. I will hold up a number and I want you to tell me what it is. (Have children count 1–10 as you hold up the sponges.) Now we are going to use these numbers to paint. Let's all go over to our Art Center and I'll show you how to do this activity. (Say the numbers as you model how to use them as stamps.)

Technology Take-Off Point

There are a wide variety of interesting number activities found at the following Web site:
http://www.topmarks.co.uk/parents/numbers.htm

Bugs in a Rug

Approximate Preparation Time

15 minutes

Learning Concept

Children make their own "Bugs in a Rug." This
activity improves children's fine-motor
coordination, their ability to follow directions,
and their mathematics readiness skills.

Materials

- ingredients and recipe for Bugs in a Rug (page 145)
- paper plates
- plastic knives
- napkins or paper towels

Warning: Ask parents if their children have any food allergies or dietary restrictions.

Lesson Preparation

Set up a Cooking Center with the recipe and ingredients for making Bugs in a Rug. Arrange children's
seating so that the lesson can be presented to the whole class or small groups. You may wish to enlist
the help of volunteers.

Remember to reproduce the recipe for the class cookbook and for the student cookbooks that will be
sent home at the end of the year.

Directed Teaching Focus

Model each step of the recipe directions for Bugs in a Rug. Allow children to make Bugs in a Rug by
imitating the steps you show.

Self-Directed Activity

Put copies of the Bugs in a Rug recipe in your Art Center for children to color and put in their
cookbooks.

What to Say

Today we are going to make a recipe with a funny name. Its called Bugs in a Rug. Some people in the
world do eat bugs, but our bugs will be raisins. (Show children the raisins.) On this table I have put
everything we need to make our recipe. Who can tell me what these things are? (Solicit responses
from children to name the items in the Cooking Center.)

Technology Take-Off Point

Try the O. Orkin Insect Zoo that is part of the Smithsonian Institution's National Museum of Natural
History. Take the virtual tour around the insect zoo at following Web site:
http://www.orkin.com/html/o.orkin.html

Bugs in a Rug Recipe

Bugs in a Rug

Ingredients

one flour tortilla

raisins

peanut butter

jelly

Directions

Spread peanut butter and jelly on a tortilla. Sprinkle with bugs (raisins) on top of the peanut butter and jelly. Roll the tortilla. Then eat the bugs in a rug.

In the Garden

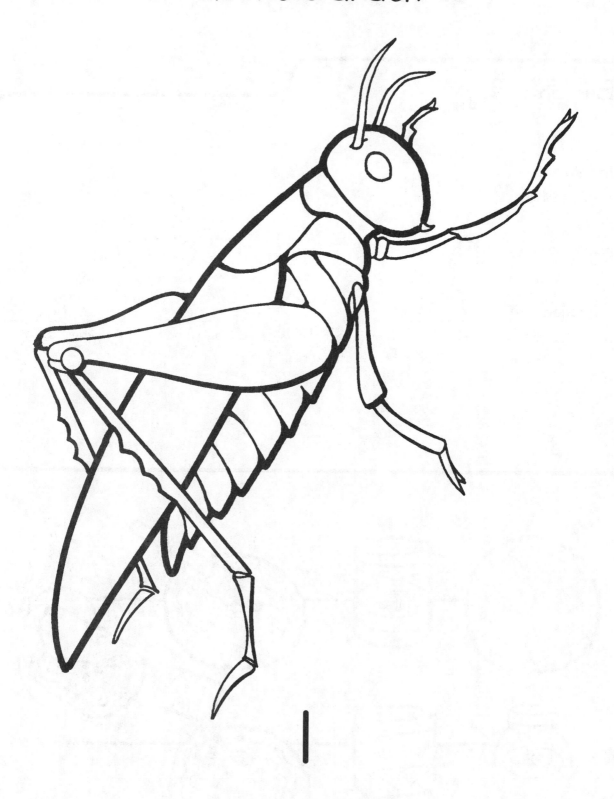

I

One Grasshopper

In the Garden *(cont.)*

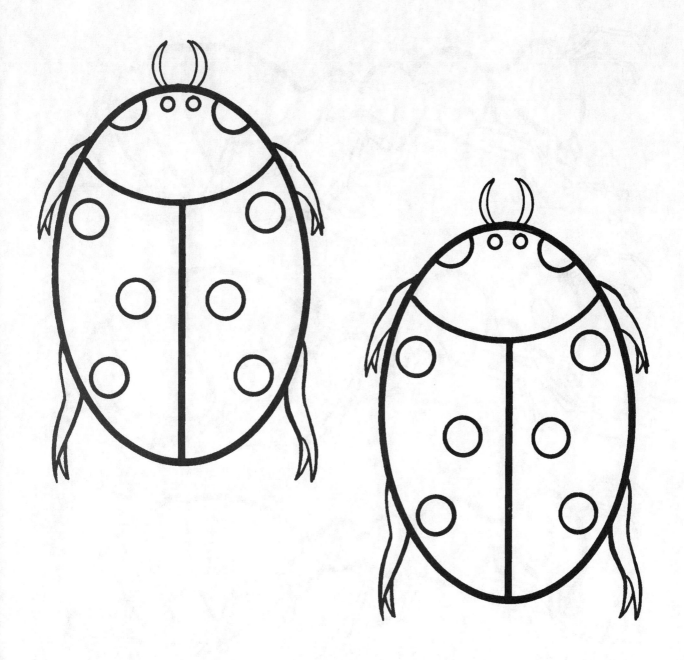

2

Two Ladybugs

In the Garden *(cont.)*

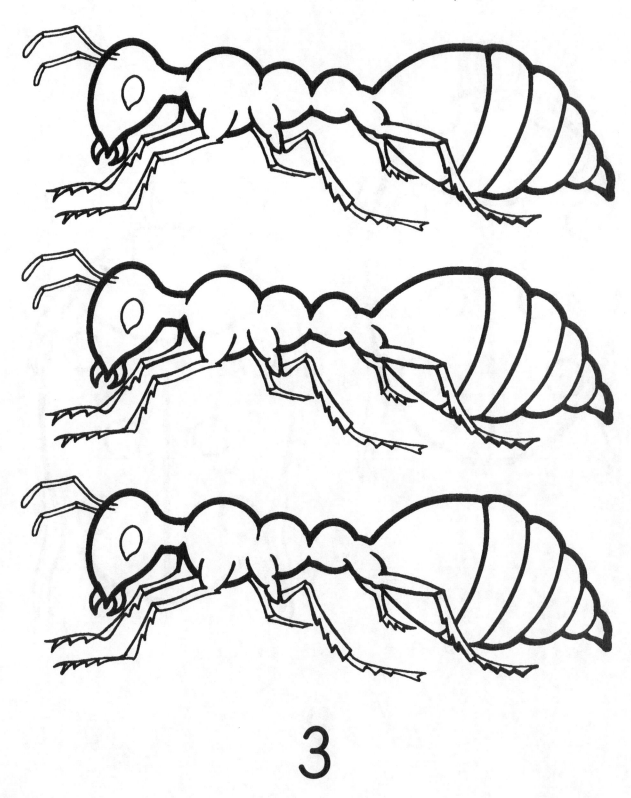

3

Three Ants

In the Garden *(cont.)*

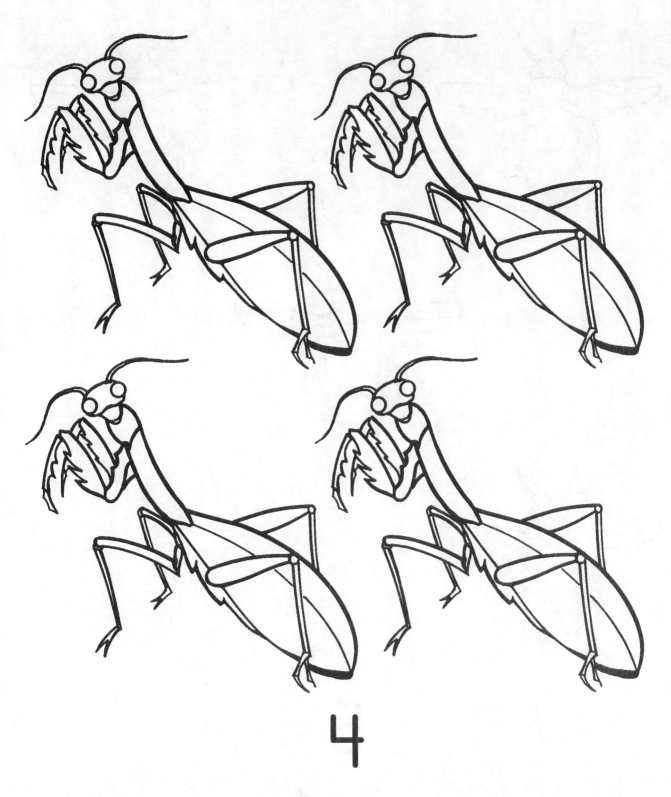

4

Four Praying Mantis

In the Garden (cont.)

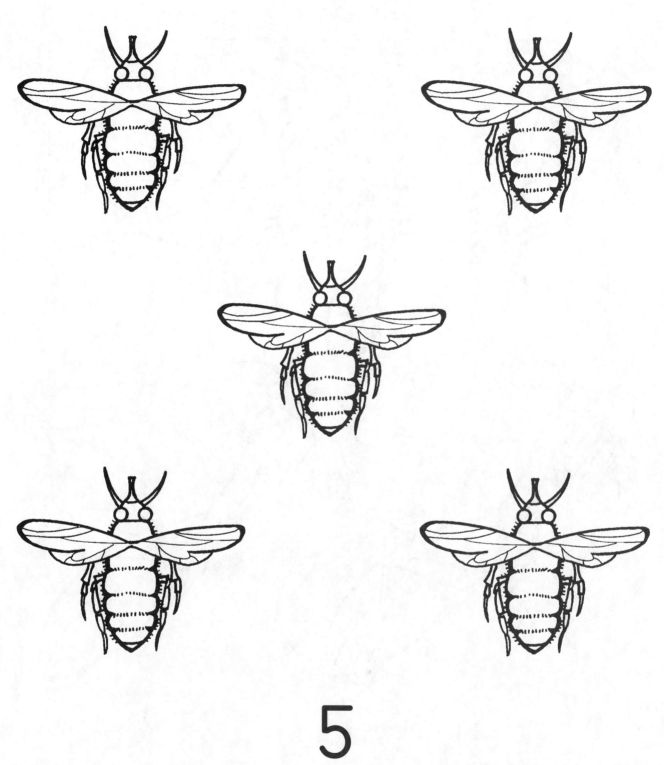

5

Five Bees

In the Garden *(cont.)*

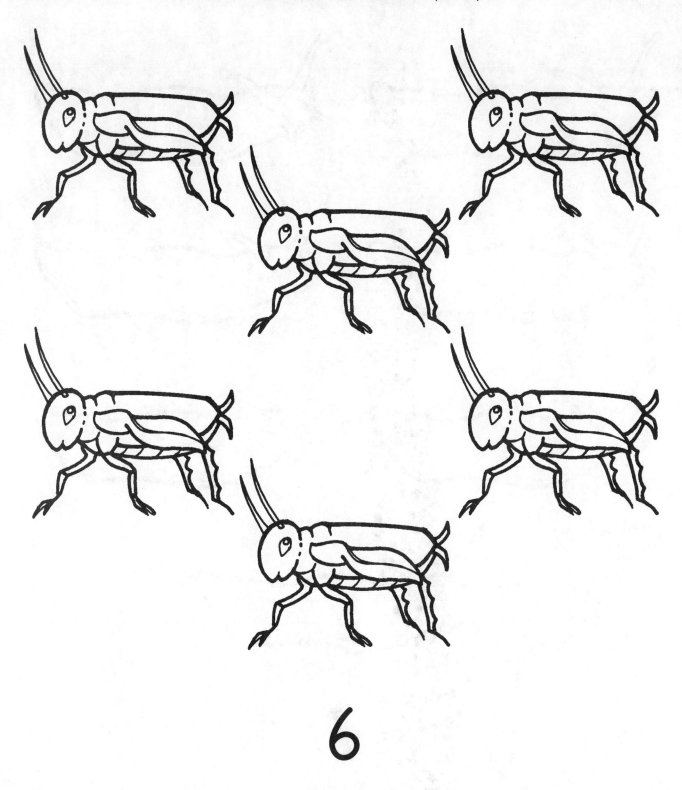

6

Six Crickets

In the Garden (cont.)

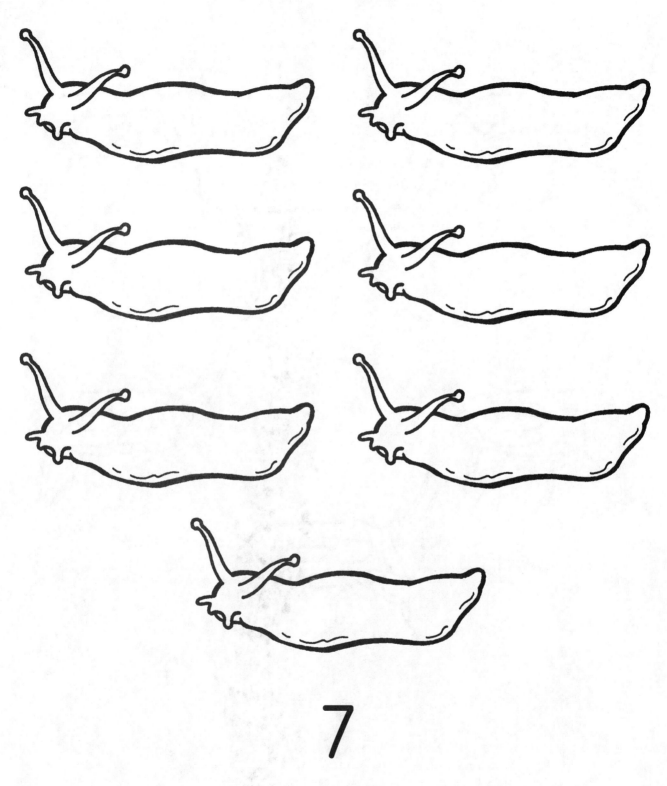

7

Seven Slugs

In the Garden *(cont.)*

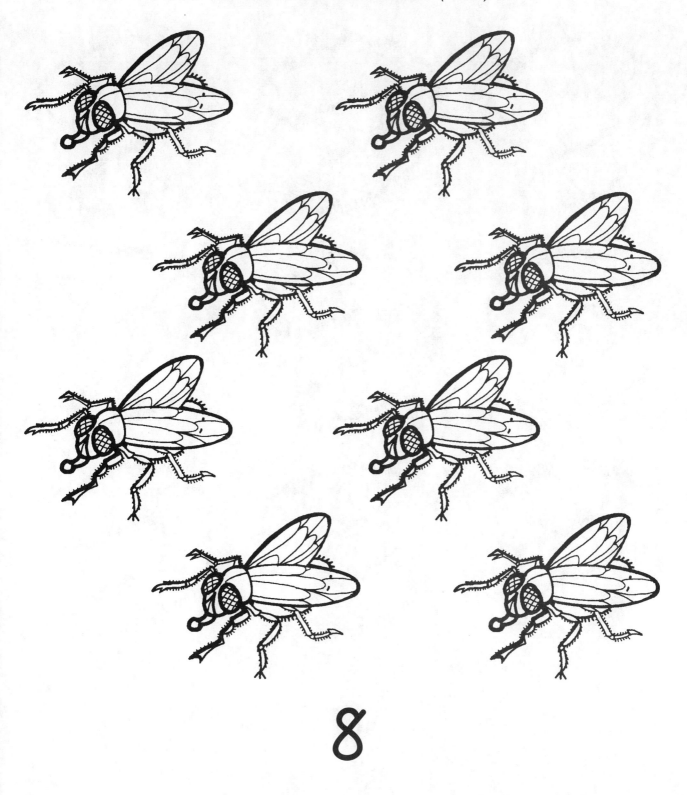

8

Eight Flies

In the Garden *(cont.)*

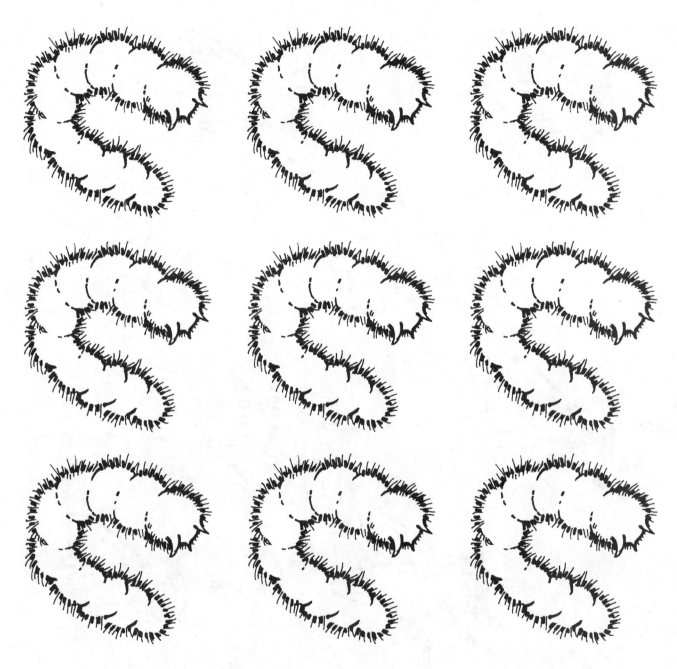

q

Nine Caterpillars

In the Garden *(cont.)*

10

Ten Butterflies

Shapes

Hands-On Internet Activities

E-Mail Shape Surprise

Shape Patrol

Thematic Activities

Art—Mr. Golden Sun Shape Picture

Cooking—Shape Sandwiches

Storybook—Hide-and-Seek Shapes

Annotated Web Sites

Alice in Wonderland

http://www.ruthannzaroff.com/wonderland/index.htm

Very young children can gain excellent mouse practice by making Alice change shapes and sizes, putting Humpty Dumpty back together again, and sending a Wonderland postcard.

KidSource Online

http://www.kidsource.com/kidsource/content/learning_math.html

This excellent resource offers lots of practical ideas to help parents and teachers help children be life-long learners in the area of mathematics. The teaching ideas show everyday activities in a mathematics context.

Time for Teletubbies

http://www.bbc.co.uk/education/teletubbies

These amazing creatures are dear to the hearts of toddlers and preschoolers. The site provides many opportunities for early learning in mathematics as children put together the shapes in a virtual jigsaw puzzle and play simple games at the Teletubbies Playground.

Billy Bear's Playground

http://www.billybear4kids.com/games/games.htm

Explore the wide variety of age-appropriate mathematics games, lessons, and links for Macintosh computer users.

Suggested Keyword Searches

educational games, educational puzzles, preschool games, preschool lessons (You may also wish to search for specific skills that children are studying.)

E-Mail Shape Surprise

Approximate Preparation Time

two hours

Learning Concept

This activity introduces children to shapes and improves their computer literacy, fine-motor coordination, and mathematics readiness.

Materials

- classroom computer
- Internet Service Provider (ISP)
- bookmarked Web sites and saved images (page 156)
- computer printer
- printer paper
- two e-mail accounts (preferred)
- Hide-and-Seek Shapes storybook (pages 163–172)

Lesson Preparation

Preview and bookmark Web sites that you intend to use with students. Save the images of shapes to disk or the hard drive. See page 304 for additional information about saving images. For each child in your class, e-mail one or more shapes as an attachment to a message.

Now set up an e-mail account for children. You may wish to use Hotmail (pages 297–300), which will allow you to set up as many free e-mail accounts as you would like. After you have established an account for children, send them e-mails with the shape image files attached.

Circle Time

Read the big book version of Hide-and-Seek Shapes to children. Review the names of the shapes shown in the book. Tell children that you have sent them an e-mail surprise.

At the Computer

Invite children use the mouse whenever possible. Begin by opening children's e-mail account. After a while, children should be able to open their own mail and attachments while you observe. After children open the attachment and view the image, print it for them or allow them to draw it. Elicit from children the name of the shapes that are shown in their attachments.

What to Say

I have sent each of you an e-mail surprise. We will open your e-mail and the attachment that is with it. Then you will tell me what your surprise shape is.

Shape Patrol

Approximate Preparation Time

one hour

Learning Concept

This activity enhances young children's computer literacy, beginning mathematics skills, and understanding of spatial relations. Children work cooperatively in groups of three.

Materials

- classroom computer
- Internet Service Provider (ISP)
- poster board or cardstock shapes, three for each child
- bookmarked Web sites (page 156)
- glue
- scissors
- craft sticks

Lesson Preparation

Preview and bookmark Web sites that you intend to use with students.

Cut out shapes (circle, square, triangle) from poster board or cardstock, making one of each shape for every child. Glue a craft stick on the back of each shape. Children may be able to help you with the gluing.

Circle Time

Begin this activity by pointing out different shapes around the classroom, focusing on circles, squares, and triangles. Tell children to hold up the appropriate shape stick to identify the shape you are pointing to in the classroom. Repeat the names of the shapes each time to help youngsters learn to connect the name with the shape. In addition, you might want to talk about each shapes attributes. Examples: Circle—A circle is round. Square—A square has four sides that are the same length. It also has four corners. Triangle—A triangle has three sides and three corners.

At the Computer

Open a bookmarked Web site and talk with children about the shapes they see at the site. Tell them to hold up the matching shape sign to show which shape they see on the computer screen. You may need to prompt children by saying such things as, "I see a circle. It is here." Point to the circle on the screen. Then say, "Hold up your circle shape sign."

What to Say

We are going use our computer to play a game called Shape Patrol. Here are three shape sticks for each of you. Let's review the names of these shapes. (Ask volunteers to name each of the three shapes—circle, square, triangle.) Now we will look at pictures of shapes on the computer. Whenever you see a shape that matches one of your shape sticks, hold up that shape stick. Here is a picture of a present. Look at the sides of the present. Hold up your shape stick if you have the shape that matches the sides of this present. (Check to see that all children raise the square.) What shape is this? (Lead children to conclude that the sides of the present are squares.)

Mr. Golden Sun Shape Picture

Approximate Preparation Time

30 minutes

Learning Concept

This activity enhances children's mathematics
knowledge and vocabulary.

Materials

- construction paper—yellow, orange, red, and black
- glue or paste
- safety scissors
- cardstock or poster board
- circle, triangle, square, and crescent patterns (page 160)
- colored felt pens
- Mr. Golden Sun Pattern (page 160)

Lesson Preparation

Prepare an Art Center for children to make their pictures. Assemble the materials you will need and
place them in the center. Trace and cut out shape patterns (page 160) from cardstock or poster board.
Create a Mr. Golden Sun model for children to see. Enlist the help of volunteers to assist children with
tracing, cutting, and gluing.

Directed Teaching Focus

You may wish to read aloud the big book version of the Hide-and-Seek Shapes storybook. Review the
names of shapes that children have learned. Then use this art experience as a follow-up activity. Show
children each shape pattern and have them repeat the name of the shape after you say it.

Self-Directed Activity

Make an extra set of shape patterns to keep in your Art Center. Then children can review the names of
shapes and trace the patterns anytime they create pictures.

What to Say

Here is Mr. Golden Sun. (Display the model that you have created.) Let's name the different shapes I
used to make Mr. Golden Sun. (Have children name the different shapes used to make Mr. Golden
Sun.) Which part of Mr. Golden Sun is a circle? (Lead students to conclude that the face is a circle.
Continue with the other shapes used to make Mr. Golden Sun.) Now you will make your own Mr.
Golden Sun.

Technology Take-Off Point

Search the Internet for sites that reinforce shape learning. After previewing the sites, pick one with
interesting photographs or pictures. Visit the site(s) with children. Ask children if they can identify
familiar shapes that are part of the various pictures.

Mr. Golden Sun Pattern

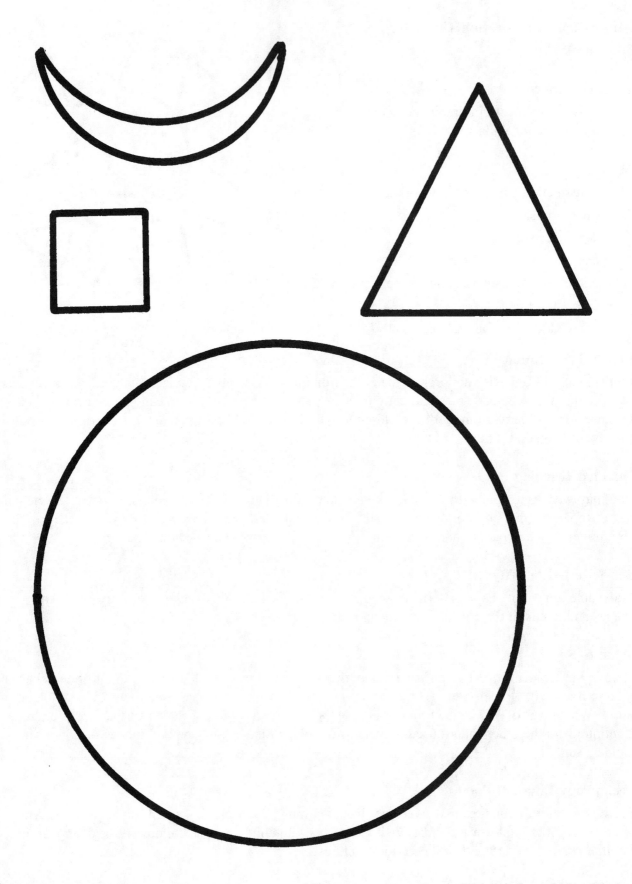

Shape Sandwiches

Approximate Preparation Time

15 minutes

Learning Concept

Making shape sandwiches reinforces the use and understanding of shapes, mathematical vocabulary, and the ability to listen to and follow directions.

Materials

- ingredients and recipe for Shape Sandwich (page 162)
- plastic knives
- paper plates
- napkins
- brown, pink, and yellow construction paper or cardstock
- laminating film and laminator or clear Contact™ paper

Warning: Ask parents if their children have any food allergies or dietary restrictions.

Lesson Preparation

Set up a Cooking Center with the recipe and ingredients for making shape sandwiches. Remember to reproduce the recipe for the class cookbook and for student cookbooks that will be sent home at the end of the year. In addition, make pretend bologna sandwiches from construction paper or cardstock. Cut out two brown squares for the bread, one pink circle for the bologna, and two yellow triangles for the cheese. Laminate the shapes or cover them with clear Contact™ paper.

Directed Teaching Focus

Tell children they will do a tasty shape activity. After you model each step, have children do the same step to make their sandwiches. Ask children to name the shapes (square, circle, triangle) that you use. Also, have them name the shape of the plates and the napkins.

Self-Directed Activity

Children can use the poster board or cardstock patterns to make pretend shape sandwiches in the classroom Home Center.

What to Say

Today we are going to make a shape sandwich that we can eat. Tell me the names of the shapes I use to make my sandwich. (Have children tell you that the slices of bread are squares, the bologna is a circle, and the cheese slice is cut into two triangles.)

Technology Take-Off Point

Visit the Kraft food site and learn what's new at Oscar Mayer. Take children on a virtual tour of the Weinermobile at the following Web site:

http://www.kraftfoods.com/index.cgi?brand_id=7

Shape Sandwich Recipe

Shape Sandwich

Ingredients

one slice of bologna

one slice of American cheese

two slices of bread

mayonnaise (optional)

Directions

If desired, spread mayonnaise on one side of each slice (square) of bread. Place the bologna (circle) on one slice of bread. Cut the cheese slice into two triangles. Place the triangles of cheese on the bologna. Place the other slice (square) of bread on top.

Hide-and-Seek Shapes

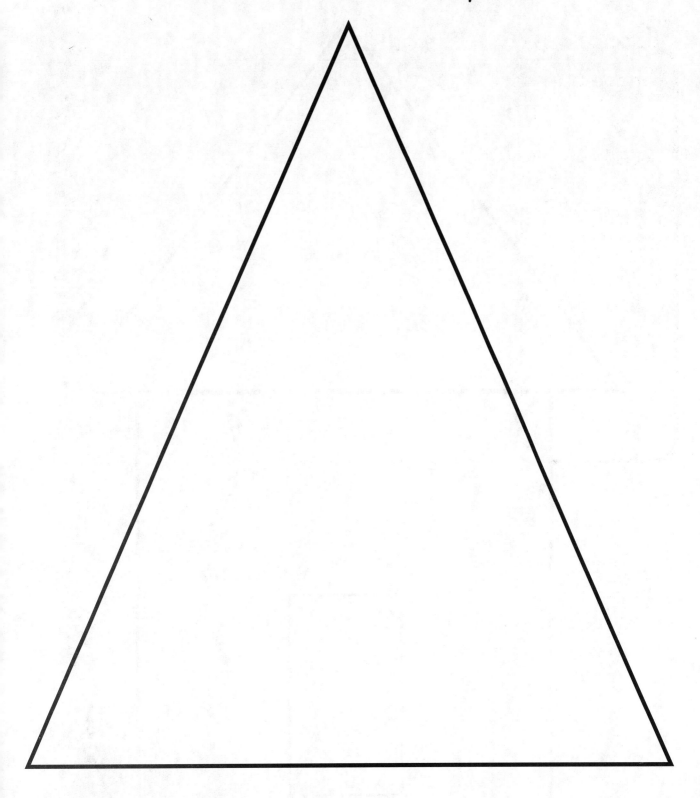

Triangle

Hide-and-Seek Shapes *(cont.)*

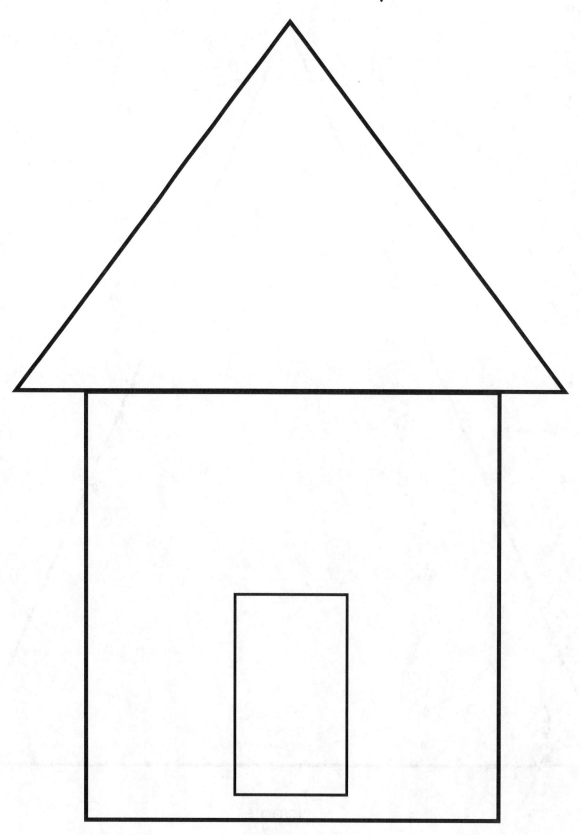

Look at the house. Where is the triangle?

Hide-and-Seek Shapes *(cont.)*

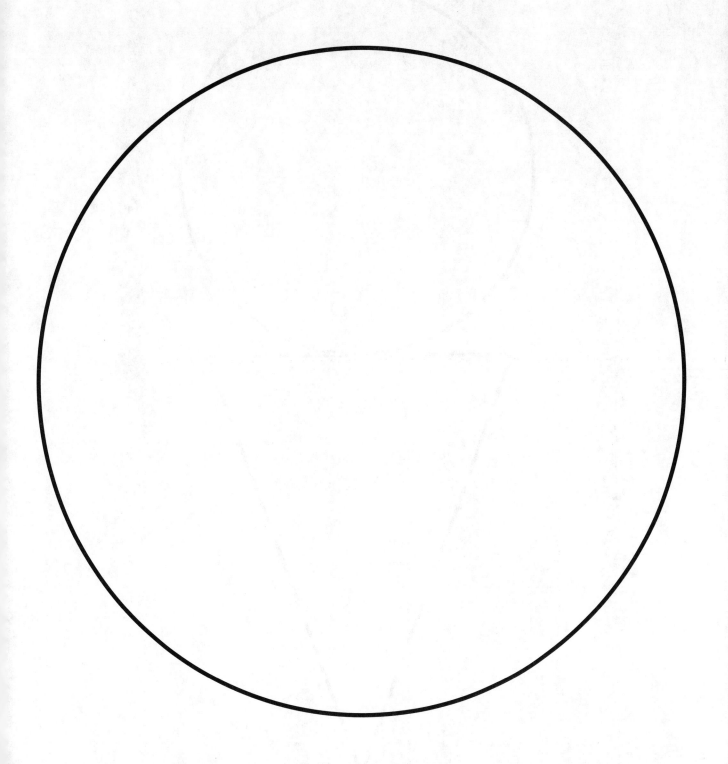

Circle

Hide-and-Seek Shapes *(cont.)*

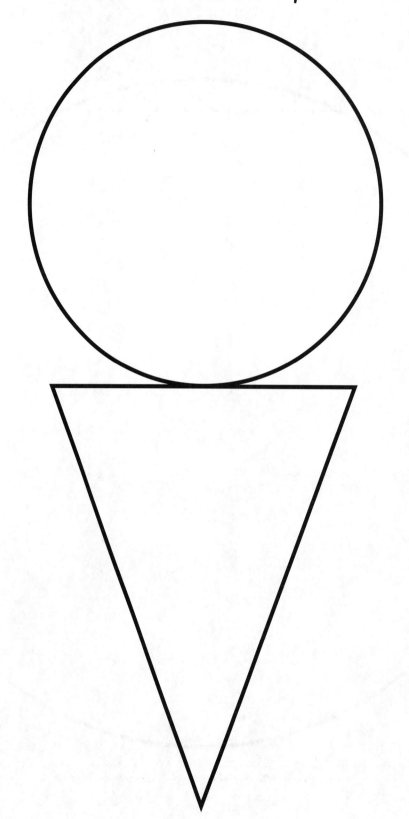

Look at the ice-cream cone. Where is the circle?

Hide-and-Seek Shapes *(cont.)*

Square

Hide-and-Seek Shapes *(cont.)*

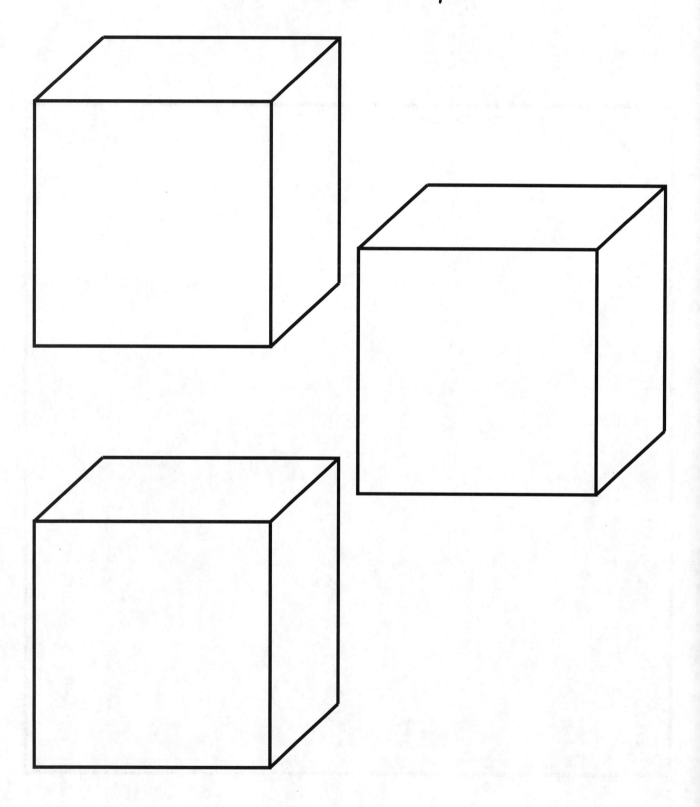

Look at the shapes. Where are the squares?

Hide-and-Seek Shapes *(cont.)*

Heart

Hide-and-Seek Shapes *(cont.)*

I Love You, Mommy!

Love Kim

Look at the Valentine. Where are the hearts?

Hide-and-Seek Shapes *(cont.)*

Rectangle

Hide-and-Seek Shapes (cont.)

Look at the books. Where are the rectangles?

172

Time

Hands-On Internet Activities

Breakfast, Lunch, and Dinner Search
Electronic Birthday Cards

Thematic Activities

Art—Paper Ring Calendar
Mathematics—How Long Is a Minute?
Cooking—Birthday Candy Cupcakes
Storybook—Benjamin Biddle's Birthday

Annotated Web Sites

Today's Date

http://www.cs.washington.edu/homes/dougz/date/

Learn more about calendars with this Web page or other links that this site suggests.

Welcome to Bry-Back Manor

http://www.geocities.com/Heartland/6459/

This site offers wonderful early childhood resources for teachers using Macintosh computers. The games are designed for young or developmentally challenged children who cannot read.

Curious George Rides the Bus

http://www.curiousgeorge.com/games/george/game/index.html

This simple game lets children help Curious George take and replace passengers' hats with a click of the mouse and reinforces one-to-one correspondence.

Owl and Mouse Educational Software

http://www.wolfenet.com/~por/foldup.html

This downloadable software for Windows 3.1 or Windows 95 allows you to print and put together a town. Adults must do much of the assembly, but preschoolers can help and then play with it. This activity highlights learning shapes.

Preschool Teacher

http://www.bv.net/~stormie/

This site was created by a preschool teacher who has compiled a wide variety of ideas in practically every subject area taught in early childhood classrooms.

Free Greeting Cards

http://www2.bluemountain.com/index.html?Id=1

This is a resource that has hundreds of links to other free card sites. Also, search using the question: *Where can I find free e-mail cards?* on **Ask.com** for additional sites.

Suggested Keyword Searches

birthday, electronic greeting cards, time, mathematics, breakfast, lunch, dinner

Breakfast, Lunch, and Dinner Search

Approximate Preparation Time

one hour

Learning Concept

Children better comprehend the times of the day as they search the World Wide Web for breakfast, lunch, and dinner foods. This activity improves young children's computer literacy, fine-motor coordination, and sequencing skills.

Materials

- classroom computer
- Internet Service Provider (ISP)
- bookmarked Web sites (page 173)
- The Land of Yummy storybook (pages 118–125; optional)

Lesson Preparation

Preview and bookmark Web sites with photo images or graphics of foods normally eaten at breakfast, lunch, or dinner. When working with children, you may wish focus on one meal per computer session so youngsters don't get overwhelmed.

Prepare a bulletin board by dividing it into three parts and labeling the sections Breakfast, Lunch, and Dinner.

Circle and Center Time

Talk with children about their favorite foods. You may wish to reread the storybook The Land of Yummy as part of the introduction to this activity. Then discuss the different types of food that children eat for breakfast, lunch, and dinner.

At the Computer

Tell children that you are going to look for _____ foods (breakfast, lunch, or dinner). Talk about the various foods children eat for that meal. Have children locate some of these foods in the bookmarked Web sites. Print some of the Internet pictures or allow children to draw pictures of the foods for the bulletin board.

What to Say

We are going to search for _____ foods on the Internet today (breakfast, lunch, or dinner). What kinds of things do you like to eat for _____ ? (breakfast, lunch, or dinner) (Allow children to name foods that they like to eat for that meal. You may wish to list these on the chalkboard or on chart paper.) Let's see if we can find pictures of some of these food on the Internet. (Have children help you use the bookmarked Web sites to locate pictures of some of the foods they named.)

Electronic Birthday Cards

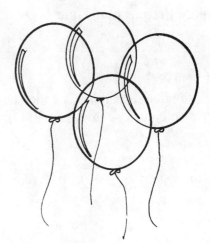

Approximate Preparation Time

one hour

Learning Concept

Children experience the thrill of receiving an
electronic birthday card made especially for
them. This activity increases young children's
computer literacy, fine-motor coordination,
vocabulary, and reading readiness skills. In
addition, it helps foster a positive self-image.

Materials

- classroom computer
- Internet Service Provider (ISP)
- bookmarked Web sites (page 173)
- two e-mail accounts (preferred)
- computer printer
- printer paper
- Benjamin Biddle's Birthday storybook
  (pages 180–194)

Note: Keep in mind that some religious groups do not celebrate birthdays. You may wish to ask
parents if their children can participate in birthday-related activities. If the issue of birthdays is a
problem, you can easily adapt this lesson by sending children general cards with messages of
encouragement. Examples: Julie, keep up the good work!—Get Well!—Thinking of You!

Lesson Preparation

Preview and bookmark Web sites that you intend to use with students. Find a site that allows you to
send free cards (page 173). Confirm every child's birthday, and write each on a large calendar. Create
an electronic birthday card for each child. If a child's birthday falls at a time when school is not in
session, send the card to be received before the weekend, holiday, or vacation. Follow the instructions
at the Web site for sending personalized cards to children in your class. Check your children's e-mail
to make sure the cards arrive when they are supposed to. Keep in mind that the cards are active for a
specific amount of time.

Circle and Center Time

Use the big book version to read Benjamin Biddle's Birthday. If you plan to celebrate children's
birthdays at school, discuss with the class the kinds of activities you will have. Be sure to provide the
same kinds of activities for all children who celebrate birthdays.

At the Computer

When it is near or on a child's birthday, tell the child to go to the computer for a special e-mail birthday
card. After children open their e-mail, allow them to print the cards to take home.

What to Say

Today is _____'s birthday. I have a surprise for _____. Let's see what it is. (Have that
child go to the computer, open the e-mail, and print the card. Remind children that everyone in your
class will get a card.)

Paper Ring Calendar

Approximate Preparation Time

30 minutes

Learning Concept

This activity increases children's understanding of time and reinforces counting skills. This art experience also enhances creativity and fine-motor coordination.

Materials

- glue or paste
- crayons
- glitter
- markers
- 1" x 8" (2.5 cm x 20 cm) strips of construction paper
- half page of construction paper, one for each child
- construction paper nametags

Lesson Preparation

Choose a holiday or school event that your class will be participating in soon (within two weeks) as the target for a calendar countdown. Create nameplates by writing each child's name on a half page of construction paper. Assemble the necessary materials in an Art Center. Arrange for a parent helper the day you make the calendars.

Directed Teaching Focus

Discuss the holiday/event that children are anticipating. Show children a real calendar and count the number of days until the holiday/event. Give each child his or her nameplate to decorate. Then give children as many construction paper strips as there are days until the holiday/event. Show children how to glue the strips into loops and connect the loops into a chain. Then help them glue the top loop onto their nameplates. Display the chains. At a certain time each day, allow children to tear a loop off their chains. After youngsters tear a loop off, have them count the remaining loops. Remind them that this is the number of days until the holiday/event.

Self-Directed Activity

Keep the material for paper-chain calendars in your Art Center so children can create calendars to countdown the days to other holidays/events.

What to Say

Let's make a calendar that shows us how many days are left until _____. (holiday/event) You will make a calendar of your own, and every day you will tear off one loop until it is the day of _____. (holiday/event)

Technology Take-Off Point

The Web site shown below is known as ***Today's Date***. It is an unbelievable resource for information about and links related to calendars.

http://www.cs.washington.edu/homes/dougz/date/

How Long Is a Minute?

Approximate Preparation Time

15 minutes

Learning Concept

This activity improves children's concept of time (seconds and minutes) and oral language skills.

Materials

- watch with a second hand, a stopwatch, or a timer
- simple timers, such as an egg timer or a kitchen timer
- various materials already found in your classroom

Lesson Preparation

Put some simple timers, such as an egg timer or a kitchen timer, in a Discovery Center.

Directed Teaching Focus

It is important to introduce time concepts long before a child can actually tell time. Show children a timekeeping device (watch, stopwatch, or timer) and talk about seconds and minutes. Illustrate how long a second and a minute are. Illustrate seconds and minutes with timed activities. Some suggestions are provided below. Compare the difference between a second and a minute and talk about how waiting several minutes can seem like a long time.

- clap hands or rest for 1 second, 5 seconds, and 10 seconds
- be silent or whisper for 15 seconds, 30 seconds, and 1 minute (60 seconds)
- stand on one foot or hop for 1 second, 15 seconds, and 30 seconds
- dance or listen to music for 10 seconds, 1 minute, and 3 minutes

Self-Directed Activity

In the Discovery Center, let children use simple timers to time their own activities.

What to Say

Today we are going to have fun with time. Let me show you how long a second is with my watch/stopwatch/timer. (Use the watch/stopwatch/timer to time one second.) Let's try a few things to get an idea of how long a second is. (Do some activities for one second. Use the suggestions listed above.) Let me show you how long a minute is with my watch/stopwatch/timer. (Use the watch/stopwatch/timer to time one minute.) Now let's do a few things to get an idea of how long a minute is. There are 60 seconds in a minute. That's like counting to 10 six times. I'll time us and tell you when we've clapped for one minute.

Technology Take-Off Point

Try a search engine designed for children (Kids Only, Yahooligans, or Ask Jeeves for Kids) to further your investigation of time.

Birthday Candy Cupcakes

Approximate Preparation Time

two hours

Learning Concept

This activity helps children understand the concept of years and reinforces math readiness skills.

Materials

- ingredients and recipe for Birthday Candy Cupcakes (page 179)
- oven
- cupcake tins
- paper baking cups
- plastic knives
- large bowl
- large spoon
- small paper plates
- napkins

Warnings: Ask parents if their children have any food allergies or dietary restrictions. Never allow children to be near the oven or to handle anything that is hot.

Lesson Preparation

Set up a Cooking Center with the recipe and ingredients for making cupcakes. If you plan to bake the cupcakes at school, arrange children's seating so that the lesson can be presented to the whole class or small groups. If you prefer not to use an oven around children, you can bring baked cupcakes for the class with the other materials. Then prepare the Cooking Center so children can frost and decorate their cupcakes.

Note: Be sure to bake a few extra cupcakes in case children drop theirs.

Remember to reproduce the recipe for the class cookbook and for the student cookbooks that will be sent home at the end of the year.

Directed Teaching Focus

Talk with children about how old they are. Introduce the concept of years in relation to their birthdays. Let children frost a cupcake. Then count with children as they put pieces of candy on top of the cupcake to match their ages.

What to Say

Today we are going to talk about how long a year is. (Show children a calendar.) There are 12 months every year. In those 12 months, there are 365 days. Every time you have a birthday, a whole year, or 365 days, has to pass until your next birthday. We will make some cupcakes. Then you will frost your cupcake and put one candy on top for every year you have been alive.

Technology Take-Off Point

Considering letting children send e-mail birthday greetings to someone they know.

Birthday Candy Cupcakes Recipe

Birthday Candy Cupcakes

Ingredients

cake mix and required ingredients as specified on the box

canned frosting

candy coated chocolates

Directions

Prepare the cupcakes according to the directions on the box. Use a plastic knife to spread canned frosting on the top of the cupcake. Place one small candy on the top of the cupcake for each year you have been alive.

Benjamin Biddle's Birthday

Benjamin Biddle was a very lucky boy. He was having a party on his birthday. He asked his mother when the party was going to be.

"In five days," said Benjamin Biddle's mother. "We have a lot to do!" she said.

Benjamin Biddle's Birthday *(cont.)*

"Five days! How long is that?" asked Benjamin. "It must be a million years from now . . . or at least a month."

"No, silly!" said Benjamin Biddle's mother. "You just have to go to bed five times. When you wake up on the fifth morning, it will be the day of your birthday party! Today we must send invitations."

Benjamin Biddle's Birthday (cont.)

Benjamin Biddle's mother took out the invitations. They had race cars on them. The invitations said, "Zoom over to my birthday party!" When Benjamin saw them, he yelled, "Zoom!"

His mother said, "Not so loud, please!"

Benjamin whispered, "Zoom." His mother smiled at him.

Benjamin and his mother wrote the invitations.

Benjamin Biddle's Birthday *(cont.)*

After Benjamin Biddle and his mother finished the party invitations, they delivered them to Benjamin's friends.

Later that night, Benjamin's mother said, "Go to bed, Benjamin. Tomorrow there will only be four days until your birthday party."

Benjamin Biddle's Birthday *(cont.)*

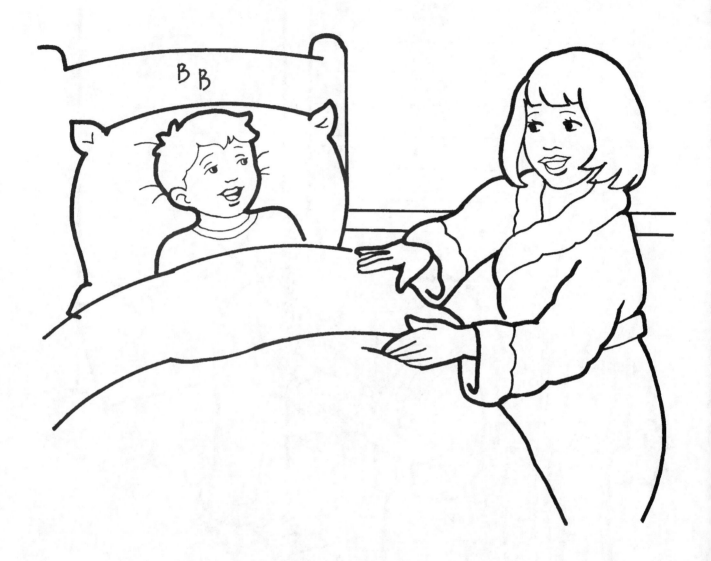

"Four days! How long is that?" asked Benjamin." It must be a million years from now. . . or at least a month."

"No, silly!" said Benjamin Biddle's mother. "You will just have to go to bed four times. When you wake up on the fourth morning, it will be the day of your birthday party! Tomorrow we must buy the decorations for your party."

Benjamin Biddle's Birthday *(cont.)*

The morning came, and Benjamin Biddle jumped out of bed. "Zoom!" he yelled. "We have a lot to do today! Today we will buy the decorations for my birthday party."

Benjamin and his mother went to the party store. Benjamin's mother asked him what kind of decorations he wanted. He decided to get plates and cups with race cars on them, a red paper tablecloth, and some big red and blue balloons.

Benjamin Biddle's Birthday *(cont.)*

Benjamin Biddle and his mother bought the decorations.

Right before Benjamin's bedtime, Benjamin's mother put the bag with the decorations in the corner of Benjamin's bedroom. His mother said, "Go to bed, Benjamin. Tomorrow there will only be three days until your birthday party."

Benjamin Biddle's Birthday *(cont.)*

"Three days! How long is that?" asked Benjamin. "It must be a million years from now. . . or at least a month."

"No, silly!" said Benjamin Biddle's mother. "You will just have to go to bed three more times. When you wake up on the third morning, it will be the day of your birthday party. Tomorrow we must make the goody bags for your party."

Benjamin Biddle's Birthday (cont.)

The morning came and Benjamin Biddle jumped out of bed. "Zoom!" he yelled. "We have a lot to do today! Today we make the goody bags for my birthday party."

Benjamin's mother asked him what kind of goodies he wanted to put in the bags. Benjamin asked for chocolate bars, taffy sticks, bubble gum, and lollipops. Benjamin Biddle and his mother went to the store and bought the goodies and some small bags.

Right before Benjamin's bedtime, Benjamin and his mother put some of the goodies in each small bag. His mother said, "Go to bed, Benjamin. Tomorrow there will only be two days until your birthday party."

Benjamin Biddle's Birthday *(cont.)*

"Two days! How long is that?" asked Benjamin. "It must be a million years from now. . . or at least a week!"

"No, silly!" said Benjamin Biddle's mother. "You only have to go to bed two more times. When you wake up on the second morning, it will be the day of your birthday party. Tomorrow we must plan the party games."

Benjamin Biddle's Birthday (cont.)

The morning came, and Benjamin Biddle jumped out of bed. "Zoom!" he yelled. "We have a lot to do today! Today is the day we plan the games for my birthday party!"

His mother asked him what kind of games he wanted. He chose the games Pin the Tail on the Donkey, Hot Potato, and Relay Races.

Benjamin Biddle and his mother listed the games on a piece of paper. They went to the store and bought Pin the Tail on the Donkey.

When it was bedtime, Benjamin's mother said, "Go to bed, Benjamin. Tomorrow there will be one day until your birthday party."

Benjamin Biddle's Birthday *(cont.)*

"One day! How long is that?" asked Benjamin. "It must be a year away. . . or at least a week!"

"No, silly!" said Benjamin Biddle's mother. "Tomorrow you will only have to go to bed one more time. When you wake up in the morning, it will be the day of your birthday party! Tomorrow we must bake your birthday cake."

Benjamin Biddle's Birthday (cont.)

The morning came, and Benjamin Biddle jumped out of bed! "Zoom!" he yelled. "Today is the day we bake my birthday cake!"

Benjamin's mother asked Benjamin what kind of cake he wanted. He decided on a chocolate cake with vanilla frosting.

Benjamin and his mother baked the cake and frosted it. Then Benjamin put a plastic red and blue race car on top of the cake.

When it was bedtime, Benjamin's mother said, "Go to bed, Benjamin. Tomorrow is the day of your birthday party!"

Benjamin Biddle's Birthday *(cont.)*

"Tomorrow! When I wake up in the morning, it will be the day of my birthday party?" asked Benjamin.

"Yes, silly!" said Benjamin Biddle's mother. "When you wake up tomorrow, it will be the day of your birthday party."

Benjamin Biddle's Birthday *(cont.)*

The morning came, and Benjamin Biddle jumped out of bed! "Zoom!" he yelled. "Today is the day of my birthday party!"

Benjamin's mother kissed him and said, "Happy birthday, Benjamin!"

Later that day Benjamin's friends zoomed over to Benjamin's house. They all had a great time at Benjamin Biddle's birthday party.

194

Guessing Games

Hands-On Internet Activities

Who Am I?

E-Mail Picture Clues

Thematic Activities

Science—Who Has the Present?

Art and Science—Fishing Pond Candy Hunt

Storybook—Tilly's Toy Box

Annotated Web Sites

Nick Jr.

http:// www.nickjr.com

These online games use Nick Jr.'s preschool programming lineup. Use these online activities for impromptu guessing games, or follow along with the television shows that many children already know and love. You will need ShockWave, but you can easily download it from the links provided.

Chalkboard

http://members.tripod.com/~Patricia_F/index.html

Developed by an early childhood educator currently teaching in the Head Start program, this site is organized by links to various themes, including a math/science link. Early childhood educators are encouraged to contact the Webmaster via e-mail.

A World of Kindergartens

http://www.iup.edu/~njyost/KHI/KHI.htmlx

The information found at this site comes from early childhood, preschool, kindergarten, and primary teachers. You can join a mailing list and harvest ideas through an alphabetical index. Make sure to check out "N" for number activities and "S" for shape activities.

Peggy's Bookmarks

http://www.iup.edu/~njyost/KHI/bookmarks.html

This link on the World of Kindergartens page deserves mention. If you don't have time to do Internet surfing for early childhood sites, let Peggy do it for you with this excellent list of links.

Cooking with Young Children

http://members.aol.com/Sgrmagnlia/index.html

This early childhood site is devoted to cooking with preschoolers. These easy recipes, including the no-heating kind, are fun and help teach children measurement and other math skills.

Suggested Keyword Searches

games, riddles, cooking, recipes, math activities, shape activities

Who Am I?

Approximate Preparation Time

one hour

Learning Concept

This activity increases young children's computer literacy and fine-motor coordination.

Materials

- classroom computer
- Internet Service Provider (ISP)
- e-mail account
- computer printer
- printer paper
- scanned pictures of children

Lesson Preparation

Scan in photographs of children, take children's pictures to be developed onto a CD-ROM, or take their pictures with a digital camera. If you use a scanner, see the user's manual for operating instructions.

Prepare a riddle about each child, with clues that will allow children in your class to guess which classmate is being described. E-mail each riddle with the child's electronic photograph attached.

Example riddle: I am four years old. I am a little girl with green eyes. My name is also the name of a flower. My seat is right next to Victor's seat. Who am I? (Daisy)

Circle and Center Time

You may wish to read aloud a version of Rumplestiltskin. Talk with children about riddles and how the clues in a riddle can help them solve it. Here are some examples you may wish to provide for children:

1. I bring mail to your house. I walk or drive a small truck. Who am I? (mail carrier; postal worker)

2. I work in a classroom and help children learn. Who am I? (teacher, teacher's aid, student teacher, principal, counselor, etc.)

At the Computer

Have children open an e-mail to read the riddle that you have sent. Allow time for children to guess who the riddle describes. Then have children open the attachment to see if they guessed the right person.

What to Say

We have an e-mail riddle. Let's read it. (Read the riddle to children. Then have children read it with you.) Who do you think that riddle is describing? (Allow time for children to guess who the riddle describes.) Let's open the attachment and look at the picture. (Say the name of the child that is shown in the picture. Confirm whether or not children have guessed the correctly to solve the riddle.)

E-Mail Picture Clues

Approximate Preparation Time

one hour

Learning Concept

This activity improves oral language and beginning mathematics skills, visual discrimination, and computer literacy.

Materials

- classroom computer
- Internet Service Provider (ISP)
- e-mail account
- bookmarked Web sites showing images of common objects found in your classroom

Lesson Preparation

Find a variety of computer images of the kinds of common objects that you have or can bring into your classroom. (Examples: television, desk, chair, chalk, chalkboard, books, pencil, pencil sharpener, clock) See page 304 for directions on how to save computer images. Preview and bookmark Web sites that you intend to use with students. Be sure all of the real objects are available in your classroom on the day of the activity.

Send yourself an e-mail with a picture of a common object attached. In the Subject textbox of the e-mail form, specify the name of a child who is to receive the e-mail. Example: This is a clue for Jeff.

Print a copy of the computer images showing the objects.

Circle and Center Time

Show children the picture of an object printed from the computer. Have them locate the real object in the classroom. Ask them to compare and contrast the picture to the real object.

At the Computer

When children are seated at the computer, open an e-mail and the attached image clue. Let the child, to whom the e-mail is written, help you manipulate the mouse and click at the appropriate times. Ask children to look carefully at the picture clue. Talk about the image and ask children to identify it. Have the child, to whom the e-mail is written, show you the real object in the classroom. Be sure that all children receive a clue at some point during this unit.

What to Say

We are going to play an Internet game called E-mail Picture Clues. A clue has been e-mailed to someone in this class. That child will help me find the clue and match it to a real object in the classroom.

Who Has the Present?

Approximate Preparation Time

30 minutes

Learning Concept

Children use visual clues to guess who is hiding a present. This activity enhances children's ability to draw conclusions as they use facts to make an educated guess.

Materials

- small presents, such as stickers or pieces of wrapped candy, one for each child

Lesson Preparation

Purchase the small presents.

Directed Teaching Focus

Model the activity with children and show them how to play. Ask each person who is IT why he or she decided to choose a particular child? Could the child who is IT tell that that classmate was holding the candy? If so, how? Talk about facial expressions and other body language clues.

Self-Directed Activity

Children can play the same guessing game using toys in your Play Center.

What to Say

Let's play a fun guessing game. I need one person to be IT and three people to be players. Each of you will get a turn to be IT and to be a player. The person who is IT will close his or her eyes, and I will give one of the other three children a present to hold behind his/her back. The other two players will only pretend they are holding the present. The person who is IT will try to guess which child is really holding the present. If you are watching the game, don't give away who is really holding the present.

Technology Take-Off Point

There are a variety of sites devoted to listing shareware. (Shareware is software that is often free or can be purchased for a modest registration fee.) Check out CNET Download.com at:
http://www.download.com/pc/list/0,339,0-d-17-329-d-,00.html?st.dl.cat17.subs.sub329 or try
http://www.download.com and follow the path—CNET: Downloads: Games: Kids.

Fishing Pond Candy Hunt

Approximate Preparation Time

one hour

Learning Concept

Children practice using eye-hand coordination, counting skills, and comparing numbers.

Materials

- ten Fish Patterns (page 200)
- five Candy Patterns (page 201)
- cardstock (various colors)
- one small magnet per fish
- one magnet for the fishing pole
- yardstick or small pole
- one-foot (30-cm) long piece of string
- glue
- laminating film and laminator or clear Contact™ paper
- blue yarn or blue butcher paper
- scissors

Lesson Preparation

Reproduce ten fish patterns and five candy patterns on cardstock. Cut out the cardstock fish and candy. On five of the fish, glue a candy on the back. Laminate the fish or use clear Contact™ paper to cover them. Glue a small magnet to the back, mouth end of each fish. Tie one end of a string to the end of a yardstick or small pole. Tie the other end of the string to a magnet. Make a pond using a circle of blue yarn or blue butcher paper. Place the fish in the pond.

Directed Teaching Focus

Model the fishing game for children. Show them that some of the fish have candy pictures on the back and some do not. Let every child practice getting a fish on the fishing line. To play, have each child catch fish. Have the class count the number of fish that are caught before the child catches one with a piece of candy on it. Use greater than and less than to compare the number of fish that children catch.

Self-Directed Activity

Have pairs of children take turns catching the fish until the pond is empty. Then tell the partners to turn over their fish and see who has the most candy pictures.

What to Say

This is our class fishpond. Let's count the fish in the pond. (Count the fish with children.) Here is a fishing pole. The fish have magnets, and so does the fishing line. Watch as I catch a fish. (Show children how to use the fishing pole to catch fish. Keep fishing until you get one with a candy glued on the back. Then show children the back of that fish and point out the candy, and explain how to play the game.)

Technology Take-Off Point

For more online games, go to the following address:

http://www.nickjr.com

Fish Patterns

Candy Patterns

Tilly's Toy Box

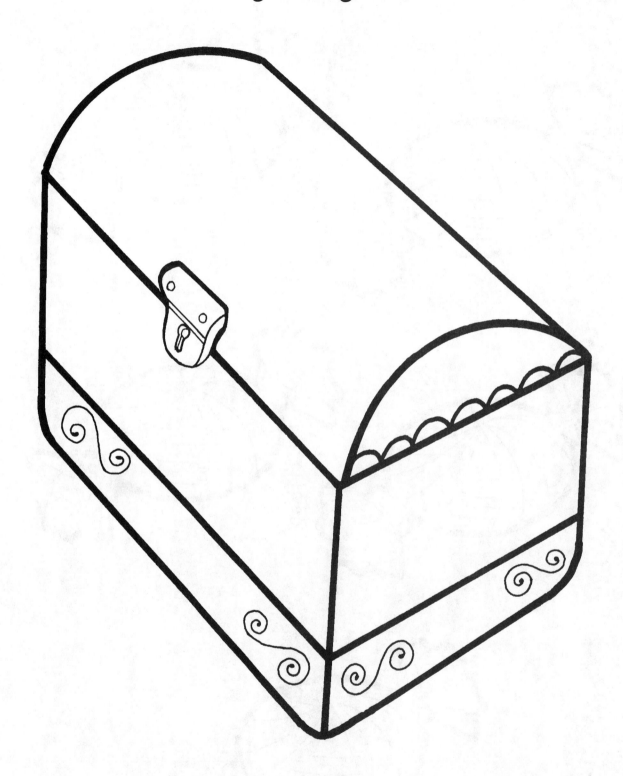

Here is Tilly's toy box. Can you guess what is inside her toy box?

Tilly's Toy Box *(cont.)*

I'm brown and fuzzy. I have a friendly face with button eyes. Tilly sleeps with me every night.

What am I?

Tilly's Toy Box (cont.)

That's right! I'm Tilly's teddy bear.

Tilly's Toy Box (cont.)

I am red and have four wheels. I go "Vroooom!" when Tilly races me around the room.

What am I?

Tilly's Toy Box (cont.)

That's right! I'm Tilly's toy car.

Tilly's Toy Box *(cont.)*

I am long and made of rope. Tilly jumps over me again and again.

What am I?

Tilly's Toy Box (cont.)

That's right! I'm Tilly's jump rope.

Tilly's Toy Box *(cont.)*

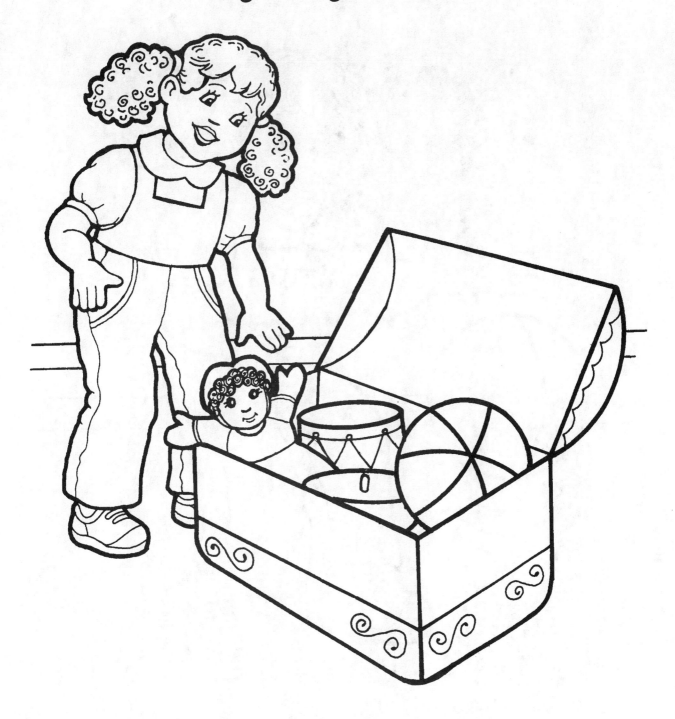

I am round and can bounce or roll. Tilly loves to throw me.

What am I?

Tilly's Toy Box (cont.)

That's right! I'm Tilly's ball.

Tilly's Toy Box (cont.)

I look like a baby, and I say, "Mama."

What am I?

Tilly's Toy Box (cont.)

That's right! I'm Tilly's doll.

Music and Instruments

Hands-On Internet Activities

Recorded Sound Effects

Listening to Music

Thematic Activities

Art—Making an Instrument

Social Studies—Sharing Songs from Home

Storybook—The Kitty Cat Band

Annotated Web Sites

K-12 Resources for Music Educators

http://www.isd77.k12.mn.us/resources/staffpages/shirk/k12.music.html

This is a very complete resource of everything anyone in elementary music education could want. While aimed at elementary school teachers, there is much here for preschool teachers who are interested in bringing music into the lives of children they teach. It features links to music resources, MIDI files, and a music search engine.

Hop Pop Town

http://www.kids-space.org/HPT/index.html

If a Web site could be a children's musical amusement park, this is it. An amazing collection of musical experiences aimed specifically at young children, this site is worth its weight in gold. There is so much to see and do, a variety of MIDI files to hear, the opportunity to make your own music, colorful characters to lead you through your musical discovery, and much more.

The Music Mania Project

http://www.ecs.edmonton.ab.ca/tlc/musicmania/

The Music Mania Project is created by teachers from all around the globe in an effort to bring music into classrooms. This site is exciting because it allows everyone to contribute to a global project on the Internet.

Jukebox-Disney MIDI Music

http://galent.com/camelot/jukbox12.htm

This site features a vast amount of Disney music MIDIs. Your class will have fun picking out favorite instrumental versions of these Disney hits. This is a great site for listening to familiar music with children.

Recorded Sound Effects

Approximate Preparation Time

two hours

Learning Concept

This activity encourages young children to explore sound. It increases young children's computer literacy, while encouraging creativity and improving listening skills.

Materials

- classroom computer
- Internet Service Provider (ISP)
- instruments and other items for sound effects
- sound recording software
- computer microphone

Lesson Preparation

Collect some or all of these things to make sound effects: tambourine, maracas, wooden blocks, bells to ring, whistles, harmonica, party noisemakers, and kazoo.

Circle and Center Time

Discuss the different sounds around the classroom and in nature. Ask children to be silent and see what they can hear. Talk about pleasant and unpleasant noises and why some people like some noises and don't like others. Talk about loud and soft noises. Have everyone whisper and yell. Let children hear each of the sound effects. Children can also create their own sound effects, such as making animal noises. Have each child choose a sound to record.

At the Computer

Follow these steps to make a sound recording:

1. For a PC, click Start. Drag to Programs, then Accessories, then Entertainment or Multimedia, and then Sound Recorder. For a MAC, click the Apple and drag to SimpleSound. The menu bar should pop up. Select Speech Quality, File, and New.
2. For a PC, the right-hand corner of the Sound Recorder is the round Record button.
3. Ask children to come right up the microphone as you click the Record button and record their sound effect. It is the same for a MAC.
4. Click File and Save As and save the recording as a sound file.
5. Play each child's sound effect back for the class to hear. For a MAC, click on the file speaker icon on your desktop to play.

What to Say

There are sounds all around us. Let's be very quiet and see what we can hear. (Discuss what children heard when they were quiet.) Okay, now let's all whisper. (Whisper.) Now let's shout. (Shout.) Which sound was loud? Which sound was quiet? Let's listen to some different sounds. Then we will use the sound recorder on our computer to record sound effects that we make.

Listening to Music

Approximate Preparation Time

two hours

Learning Concept

This activity introduces young children to music on the Internet.

Materials

- classroom computer
- Internet Service Provider (ISP)
- bookmarked Web sites with downloadable sound clips (page 213)

Lesson Preparation

Preview Web sites with downloadable audio files that you intend to use with students. Download and save the audio files. Then minimize them on your desktop. This way there is no waiting time and children can listen to the music immediately.

Note: If you have trouble playing various sound files on a MAC, download the freeware version of SoundApp, a software designed to play a variety of sound file formats that MACs do not usually play. You can find it at **http://macdownload.com**.

Circle and Center Time

This portion of the activity will change every time you listen to audio files. For example, if you are interested in hearing a MIDI file from a movie soundtrack, you may wish to view a portion of the film before you begin that particular hands-on session.

At the Computer

Invite children to sit at the computer and open your media player to listen to the music files. Your PC or MAC has a sound player, but you can also download a player such as Real Player from the Web. Have children listen to the various files you select, and see if they have favorites. As an alternative, you can allow children to select songs they know.

What to Say

We are going to hear some audio files on the computer today that I have downloaded from the Internet. (Tell children what kind of audio files they are going to hear. If you play music with which children are familiar, ask them to name the tune or sing along with the audio file.)

Making an Instrument

Approximate Preparation Time

one hour

Learning Concept

This activity enhances an understanding of music production, artistic ability, listening skills, and the ability to following directions. In addition, children learn how materials can be reused.

Lesson Preparation

Gather the materials needed to make all the instruments. Preview and bookmark Web sites that have music and musical instruments. Remember that you can save sound files to disk for later use.

• •

Tissue Box String Instrument

Materials

- empty tissue box
- three rubber bands
- markers, poster paints and paintbrushes, or construction paper and glue

Directions

1. Decorate the tissue box in one of the following ways: color with markers, paint with poster paints, or glue on pieces of construction paper.
2. Stretch the rubber bands around the box, and over the opening in the center. Place the rubber bands so they are not touching each other.
3. Strum the fingers across the rubber bands where they cross the center of the tissue box.

• •

Wrapping Paper Roll Rain Stick

Materials

- empty wrapping paper roll
- butcher paper
- tape
- dry rice
- markers, poster paints and paintbrushes, or construction paper and glue

Directions

1. Decorate the wrapping paper roll in one of the following ways: color with markers, paint with poster paints, or glue on pieces of construction paper.
2. Cover one end of the roll with butcher paper and secure with tape.
3. Take a long strip of butcher paper and fold it back and forth in one-inch (2.5 cm) increments to make a zigzag pattern. Turn the tube so the covered end is facing the floor. Insert the folded paper in the tube. This creates a pathway to make the rice pour through the tube more slowly, creating a rain sound effect.
4. Pour one cup (250 mL) of dry rice into the wrapping paper roll.
5. Cover the open end of the roll with butcher paper and secure with tape.
6. To hear the rain sound effect, hold the tube in one hand and gently flip it up and down by twisting the wrist.

Making an Instrument *(cont.)*

●●

Coffee Can Drum

Materials

- coffee can with lid
- poster paint and paintbrush
- glue
- large piece of fabric
- large rubber band

Directions

1. Paint the coffee can. Allow the paint to dry.
2. Glue the lid onto the can. Allow the glue to dry.
3. Cut a piece of fabric that is large enough to fit over the lid and hang down about 2" (5 cm) over the can. Tightly stretch the fabric over the lid.
4. Hold the fabric in place with the rubber band. Be sure the rubber band is close to the lid.

●●

Directed Teaching Focus

Introduce this activity by discussing the different kinds of instruments that children might have seen or heard. Use the Internet to introduce children to various kinds of music and musical instruments.

Set up instrument-making center in which all of the materials are placed. You may wish to enlist the help of parent volunteers. After instruments are completed, have an impromptu jam session. March around your school to give a marching band performance.

Self-Directed Activity

After the instruments are completed, leave them in a Music Center for children to use whenever they wish.

What to Say

We are going to learn about different kinds of musical instruments. Let's talk about the ones you might already know. (Lead a discussion, allowing children to tell about musical instruments that they have heard or seen.) Now let's go to a few Internet Web sites to listen to some interesting music. Try to listen for the different kinds of instruments. (After listening to the music, direct children's attention to the Music Center.) Now we are all going to make an instrument of our own. You can see that I have made a drum out of a coffee can. Show students the coffee can drum. Then show them the wrapping paper tube rain stick.) This is a rain stick made from a wrapping paper tube. (Show them the tissue box string instrument.) This string instrument, which is like a guitar, is made from a tissue box.

Technology Take-Off Point

Consider recording children playing their instruments. While your new hand-made instruments might not be very musical, they will certainly produce sounds for the sound effect activity (page 214).

Sharing Songs from Home

Approximate Preparation Time

one hour

Learning Concept

This activity enhances dramatic play, social skills, memorization, and singing ability.

Materials

- Classroom Songfest Parent Letter
  (page 220), one for each child
- Songfest Book Form (page 221),
  one for each child
- tape recorder and blank cassette tapes
- blocks
- red, yellow, and orange construction paper

Lesson Preparation

Reproduce the parent letter and song form. Send these home to parents.

Directed Teaching Focus

Begin this activity by talking with children about songs that they know. You may already sing songs in class on a daily or weekly basis. Begin by singing the songs your class knows and then introduce the idea of a songfest. Explain to the class that each child will have the chance to share his or her favorite song at the songfest. Point out that each child will need to decide on a song to share and practice singing that song with his or her family the week before the songfest.

Send home the parent letter, which explains the activity to parents, and the songbook form, which allows parents to write the lyrics to the song that their child will sing at the songfest. Collect the forms that are returned and collate them into a songbook that you can reproduce. Allow children to take home their Class Songbooks.

Prepare your classroom for the songfest by building a pretend campfire out of blocks and red, yellow, and orange construction paper in the middle of your circle. Ask children to sit cross-legged around the "campfire" for the songfest.

Invite parent volunteers to take part in the songfest and share their favorite songs if they would like to do so. Remember to tape record the festivities. Later, you can use the tape to make a sound file on your computer.

Sharing Songs from Home *(cont.)*

Self-Directed Activity

Make a Singing Center with a tape recorder and blank tapes for children to record themselves singing. Save the best for children to hear again and again by punching out the plastic protection tabs on the back of the cassette.

What to Say

I know that everyone in our class likes to sing because we sing every day. Who can think of a song we sing? (Ask a volunteer to name a song.) Okay, let's begin by singing that song. (Lead the class in singing that song.)

This week, I want each of you to think of your favorite song and practice it at home. Your family can help you pick a song. Then next week you can share your song with the class at a songfest. On the day of the songfest, we will pretend that we are sitting around a campfire. Then we will sing all of your songs. Right now I am going to give you two papers. The first one is a letter to tell your parents about our songfest activity. The second one is for your parents to write the words to the song you have chosen to share. After our songfest, we will make a class songbook with the words to your favorite songs. You will get to take the songbook home to share with your family.

Technology Take-Off Point

Use the Sound Recorder feature of Windows 95 or better or MAC's SimpleSound to record sound files using your cassette tape of the songfest. These sound files can e-mailed to parents who give you permission to do so. Use the following steps to create a sound file:

1. Use a cassette tape recorder to record children singing.
2. Plug in your computer microphone, or position the tape recorder near the built-in microphone on your computer.
3. For a PC, click Start, drag to Programs, then Accessories, then Entertainment or Multimedia, and then Sound Recorder. For a MAC, click the Apple and drag to SimpleSound. Remember the menu bar becomes your application's menu bar. Select Speech Quality, File, and New.
4. Click on the Record button on Sound Recorder or Simple Sound as you begin the taped version of children singing.
5. Click on the Stop button on Sound Recorder or Simple Sound when the recording of the song is over.
6. Then, for a PC or MAC, click on File and then Save As. The Save As dialog box will appear.
7. For a PC, save the sound file to a disk or a folder on your hard drive. For a MAC, save the sound file to a disk, your desktop, or a folder on your hard drive. Remember to give each file a name that is easily recognizable so you can easily find it again later.
8. Click Save.

Classroom Songfest Parent Letter

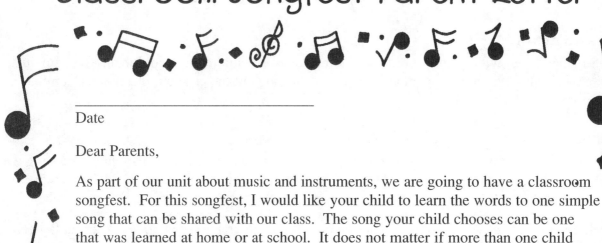

_____
Date

Dear Parents,

As part of our unit about music and instruments, we are going to have a classroom songfest. For this songfest, I would like your child to learn the words to one simple song that can be shared with our class. The song your child chooses can be one that was learned at home or at school. It does not matter if more than one child shares the same song with our class. The important thing is that every child will have the opportunity to share a song.

You may wish to teach your child one of the following songs, or pick one that you already enjoy singing together.

- Row, Row, Row Your Boat
- Jingle Bells
- Rudolph the Red Nose Reindeer
- Happy Birthday
- This Old Man
- Ba, Ba, Blacksheep
- Where is Thumbkin?
- Yankee Doodle

- Are You Sleeping?
- Twinkle, Twinkle, Little Star
- The Alphabet Song
- If You're Happy and You Know It
- Rock-a-Bye Baby
- Take Me Out to the Ballgame
- The Wheels on the Bus

Please help you child practice the song he or she has chosen. Your child should be prepared to share this song at our songfest on _____ . Remember, this singing activity is just for fun; your child's performance does not have to be perfect.

Thank you for helping your child prepare for this activity. If you have any questions or you would like volunteer to help in our class for this or any other activity, please feel free to call me.

Sincerely,

_____
Teacher

_____
School

_____
Phone

Songfest Book

Directions: Please write down the words to the song that your child learns so we can make a class songbook. Thank you.

Child's Name: _____

Song Title: _____

Words to the Song:

_____

_____

_____

_____

_____

_____

_____

_____

_____

_____

_____

_____

_____

_____

_____

The Kitty Cat Band

The Kitty Cat Band came to play one night,

Came to play by the light of the moon.

They played while I tried to go to sleep,

So I heard each kitty cat tune.

The Kitty Cat Band *(cont.)*

Each cat played a different instrument,

Making music I'd never heard.

The Kitty Cat Band came to play one night,

I heard them—you have my word.

The Kitty Cat Band (cont.)

The biggest cat played the piano.

He used his front paws on the keys.

His kitty cat friend sang loud and clear,

A song as sweet as you please.

224

The Kitty Cat Band (cont.)

The next kitty cat played a guitar,

Strummity, strum, she strummed.

She sang country songs in a lovely voice,

As I stood by my window and hummed.

The Kitty Cat Band (cont.)

The next cat played a trombone.

I peeped through my window and saw

Him moving the slide up and down—

Using only his little white paw.

The Kitty Cat Band *(cont.)*

The last kitty cat played some drums—boom, boom!

And a cymbal that went crash, crash!

I stood at my window in the light of the moon.

When my door opened, I made a mad dash.

The Kitty Cat Band (cont.)

I jumped into bed as my mother walked in.

She said, "Honey, is that music I hear?"

I said, "I think it's a cat in the yard.

Or maybe an owl, or a deer."

228

The Kitty Cat Band (cont.)

I really knew, but I didn't tell her.

They were there every night like they planned.

Those musical cats with their instruments—

Those cats in the Kitty Cat Band!

Dance and Movement

Hands-On Internet Activities

Movement Photos from Home

Watching Movement Video Clips

Thematic Activities

Social Studies—Dance Party

Art—Movement Flags

Storybook—Watch Me Move

Annotated Web Sites

The Bob Macke Dance Company

http://members.aol.com/bmac5175/choreography.html

If you are interested in sharing with children some tap dancing video and sound clips, this is the place to start. There are a wide variety of tap combinations, most with sound and video clips.

Dance Resource Index

http://wwar.com/dance/index.html

This site includes anything and everything about dance. It is a resource that you will want to bookmark so you can explore literally hundreds of dance links. The resources are organized into specific dance styles. Then each main link has anywhere from one to several hundred secondary links for that specific style of dance.

Just Feet

http://www.bromley.ac.uk/jtu/improv/

This site has been designed by a tap dancer. At this site you will find lots of information about the Web site creator's perspective on tap dancing and a very interesting AVI file that shows his feet while he is dancing. This is an interesting site that your students will enjoy.

Dance in Mexico

http://www.geocities.com/Vienna/1854

This site features information about dance in Mexico. The text is provided in both English and Spanish. Rich in photographs, this site can give your children a look at dance in a country other than the United States. This site is well worth a look from the perspective of introducing children to another culture.

Suggested Keyword Searches

dancers, dance, music (You may also wish to search for a specific type of music or dance.)

Movement Photos From Home

Approximate Preparation Time
one hour

Learning Concept
This activity increases young children's fine-motor
coordination and thinking skills.

Materials

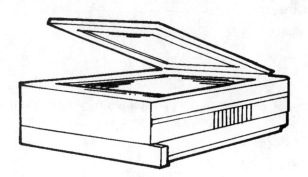

- classroom computer
- Internet Service Provider (ISP)
- scanner
- Parent Letter (page 232), one for each child
- photograph, one of each child
- Watch Me Move storybook (pages 236–239)

Lesson Preparation

Reproduce the parent letter and send it home with children. Have children bring to class a photograph
that shows them moving. If some children do not have any photographs at home or their parents do not
want to send any of their photographs to school, arrange to take children's movement pictures at school.

Review the instruction manual to learn how to operate the scanner if you do not already know how.

Circle Time

To introduce this activity, read the Watch Me Move storybook. Then let each child show his or her
photograph to the class and describe the movement that is shown in it.

At the Computer

Scan each child's photo and save the image to a disk or your hard drive. Children will be fascinated as
they watch their photographs being scanned. Allow children to view their scanned images on the
computer screen.

What to Say

We are going to put each of your photographs on the scanner. The scanner will copy the picture so that
we can look at it on the computer. Let me show you how the scanner works. (Demonstrate how to
scan a photograph.) Now that we have scanned this photo, let's take a look at it on the computer
screen. (Show children the image on the computer. Then hold up the photograph next to the computer
screen.) Let's look at the photograph while we look at the picture on the computer. (Ask children to
compare and contrast the photograph and the computer image.) How are the computer image and the
photograph different? How are they the same?

Parent Letter

_____

Date

Dear Parent,

Our class is studying a unit on movement and dance. If possible, please send a photograph of your child doing some kind of activity. The kinds of activities your youngster might be doing in the photographs include:

- dancing
- running
- swimming
- jumping
- hiking
- ice skating
- riding a bicycle
- roller-skating or roller-blading
- using playground equipment
- playing a game or sport

You do not need to take a special photograph for this lesson. Simply locate a photograph that you already have. If you are unable to send a photograph of your child to school, please let me know and I will arrange to take a photograph of your child at school. Please feel free to call me if you have any questions.

Thank you for your help in this matter.

Sincerely,

_____

Teacher

_____

School

_____

Phone

Watching Movement Video Clips

Approximate Preparation Time
two hours

Learning Concept
This activity increases children's awareness of movement and dance.

Materials
- classroom computer
- Internet Service Provider (ISP)
- bookmarked Web sites with downloadable video clips (page 230)

Lesson Preparation
Preview Web sites with downloadable video clips that you intend to use with the children. Download and save the video clips. Then minimize them on your desktop. This way there is no waiting time and children can see the video clips immediately.

Your PC or MAC operating system will open a video file in a media player available on your computer, but you can also download a player such as Real Player from the Internet.

Circle and Center Time
This portion of the lesson will change every time you view a different video clip. Examples: If you are viewing a clip of a ballet dancer, you might want to check out a library book that tells about ballet and shows pictures of ballet dancers. You might also show children real objects associated with ballet such as a pair of ballet shoes and a tutu. Read the book to children before moving to the computer. If you are showing a video clip of exercises, then you can begin with a general book about exercise and fitness. If you are showing a video clip about a particular sport, read a book about that sport or a biography about an athlete who plays that sport. Be sure the books that you read aloud to children are easy enough for them to understand and have a number of photographs or illustrations that show movement.

At the Computer
Invite children to sit at the computer and open up your media player to view the video clips. Allow children to watch the clip of the dance or movement on the computer. Then step away from the computer and encourage children to imitate the movement or dance they saw.

What to Say
Today I'm going to start our lesson by reading a book about _____ . (Tell children what type of movement is described in the book you have chosen to read aloud.) Then we are going to see a video clip on our computer that I have downloaded from the Internet. (Tell children what type of movement is shown in the clip before showing it to the class. Read the book. Then show the clip. Lead a discussion about the kind of movements described in the book and shown in the video clip.) Now let's move to the middle of our classroom and try doing the movement we saw on our computer. (Make sure children have plenty of room to move without running into each other.)

Dance Party

Approximate Preparation Time

30 minutes

Learning Concept

This activity increases gross- and fine-motor coordination and enhances creativity and listening skills.

Materials

- radio; tape, record, or CD player
- music on cassette tapes, records, or CDs (optional)
- timer

Lesson Preparation

Preparing for this activity is as simple as can be. Designate a dancing space and play some music. You can make this activity more involved by using various kinds of music, or you can just turn on the radio and have children dance around to the music.

Directed Teaching Focus

Present a certain kind of music. Ask children to share any dance styles they might already know. Lots of small children take lessons, or have siblings that have taught them some dance moves. Then let everyone dance. Set a timer to indicate the end the dance session, then move on with your next activity.

Self-Directed Activity

Let children have their own designated dance area. Stock the area with some music that children can play for themselves. The easiest thing for children to use is cassette tapes and a tape player. Some tape players are specifically made for children, meaning they are almost indestructible. Encourage children to move to the music during self-directed play.

What to Say

Today we are going to have fun dancing. What is your favorite song to dance to? (Allow children to respond. You may wish to ask children if they have a favorite singing group, singer, or type of music to dance to.) Let's try dancing to some music I play for you. (Before starting the music, be sure children have plenty of room to dance without running into each other.)

Technology Take-Off Point

As you look at the various dance sites in Annotated Web Sites (page 230), keep track of all the different kinds of dance styles you see on the Internet. Print a picture from each site for a dance bulletin board or make laminated dance flash cards so children can name the different types of dance such as ballet, tap, and modern.

Movement Flags

Approximate Preparation Time

30 minutes

Learning Concept

This activity enhances creativity, artistic ability, gross- and fine-motor coordination, and listening skills.

Materials

- empty paper towel tubes, one for each child
- long pieces of ribbon or crepe paper
- poster paint and paintbrushes, markers, or crayons

- tape or staples and stapler
- radio; tape, record, or CD player
- music on cassette tapes, records, or CDs (optional)

Lesson Preparation

Prepare for this activity by collecting the empty paper towel tubes. You may find that you can get these in a few days by asking for parents to send the empty tubes to school with children. Then put together an Art Center for making the movement flags. You may wish to paint the tubes and let them dry thoroughly before beginning the activity with children, or you can simply provide markers or crayons for children to decorate the tubes.

Next use tape or staples to attach several long pieces of ribbon or crepe paper to one end of each paper towel tube. The ribbon or crepe paper strips should sail around gracefully as the child moves the paper towel tube back and forth in the air.

Directed Teaching Focus

Model for the class how to make a movement flag. After children decorate their empty paper towel tubes, help them attach the ribbons or crepe paper strips. Select some music and invite children to use their flags as they move to the music. You may wish to model a few ways that children might move with the flags or leave it totally to their own imaginations. Vary what happens by changing the style and tempo of the music you play.

Self-Directed Activity

Allow children to listen to music and move their flags to the beat.

What to Say

Today we are going to make special movement flags that we can use when we move to music. I will show you how to make one. (Demonstrate how to make the flag. Then help children make their own. You may wish to show how to move the flag.) Now I will play some music so you can move your flag as you move or dance. (Be sure children have plenty of room to move their flags without running into each other.)

Technology Take-Off Point

Take pictures of this activity to scan and save on your computer.

Watch Me Move

Watch me hop like a bunny, leap like a panther, and jump like a horse.

Can you hop, leap, and jump like me?

Watch Me Move *(cont.)*

Watch me crawl like a bug, a kitten, and a baby.

Can you crawl like me?

Watch Me Move *(cont.)*

Watch me spin like a windmill, a top, and a ballerina.

Can you spin like me?

Watch Me Move *(cont.)*

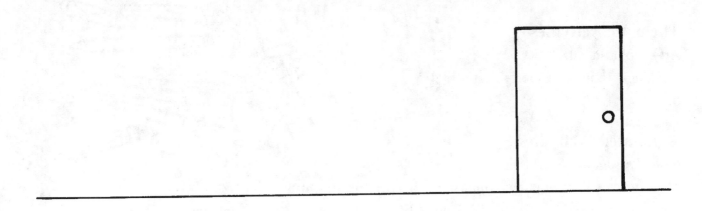

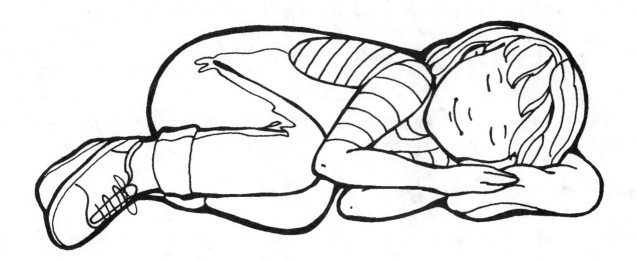

Watch me drop to the ground and take a rest.

Can you rest like me?

Art

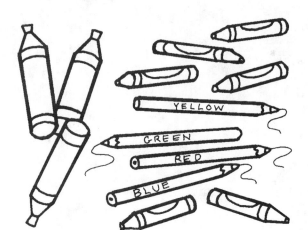

Hands-On Internet Activities

Children's Virtual Art Gallery

Coloring Online

Thematic Activities

Art—Color Palette

Cooking—Rainbow Colors Gelatin

Storybook—I Can Color!

Annotated Web Sites

CyberPreschool

http://www.americatakingaction.com/cyberpre/funsites.htm

This site, sponsored by America Taking Action, is chock-full of interesting experiences and activities for the preschool set. An interesting part of the home page is that it is a link for public and private schools across the nation with plenty of opportunities for people to get involved by sharing information in their own state and city.

Gayle's Preschool Rainbow—Activity Central

http://www.preschoolrainbow.org/preschool-fall.htm

If you would like to get a fresh approach on a variety of preschool arts-and-crafts activities, as well as a number of other interesting developmentally appropriate activities for youngsters, consider accessing this resource.

Crayola Art Education

http://education.crayola.com/

This interesting site offers art information and ideas for educators. A variety of links lead you to various crayon-related information. You may wish to send in your favorite lesson plans to try your chance at winning some wonderful prizes.

Linkopedia—Children's Coloring Books

http://www.linkopedia.com/kids_coloringbooks.html

This site has many links to lots of great coloring sites, including Barney's official Web site, Kellogg's, Sesame Street, and more. This site provides both coloring pages and online coloring activities.

Suggested Keyword Searches

art, artists, art education, art galleries, colors, coloring activities (You may also wish to search for specific artists and types of art.)

Children's Virtual Art Gallery

Approximate Preparation Time

two hours

Learning Concept

This activity enhances children's artistic ability,
fine-motor coordination, self-esteem,
and self-awareness.

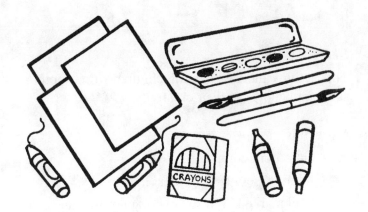

Materials

- classroom computer
- Internet Service Provider (ISP)
- scanner
- art supplies (varies, depending on the type of artwork done)

Lesson Preparation

Begin by deciding what kind of art children will create. Even a crayon picture will work well. Set up
an Art Center with the necessary supplies.

Review the instruction manual to learn how to operate the scanner if you do not already know how.

Note: Be sure the art that children create will be flat and will easily fit on your scanner. In addition, do
not have children create artwork using supplies, such as chalk or pastels, which might damage your
scanner. As an alternative to scanning the artwork itself, you may wish to consider making color
photocopies first and then scanning the copies.

Circle Time

Explain to children that they will be creating artwork that will be put in a classroom art gallery on the
computer. Explain the art project itself and, as children finish their artwork, move to the computer for
the hands-on portion of this activity.

At the Computer

After children finish their artwork, let them watch you scan the art. As the class views each picture on
the computer, show the real artwork next to the computer. Ask children to compare and contrast the
real artwork with the computer images.

You may wish to e-mail children's artwork to parents who have given you permission to do so.

What to Say

We are going to make pictures today. Then we will scan your pictures so that we can save the images
on our computer. You can see how your artwork looks as a computer image. (After scanning in the
artwork, show each real picture as you display its computer image. Invite children to compare and
contrast the picture with the computer image. Do this for each child's piece of art.) How are the
computer image and the piece of art different? How are they the same?

Coloring Online

Approximate Preparation Time

two hours

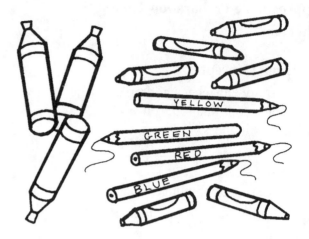

Learning Concept

This activity increases young children's fine-motor skills and enhances their creativity.

Materials

- classroom computer
- Internet Service Provider (ISP)
- bookmarked Web sites with coloring pages, online and/or printable (page 240)
- crayons, markers, or colored pencils

Lesson Preparation

Preview Web sites with coloring pages (online and/or printable) that you intend to use with students. When you are selecting sites, find simple pictures that you think will work well for your students. There is no way to tell which sites will be favorites until children have a chance to try them.

Online coloring is an interesting computer mouse and coloring exercise in which a child clicks on a color from a color pallet to fill in sections of a outline picture. Printable coloring pages are outline pictures that can be printed for children to color using traditional methods such as crayons, markers, or colored pencils.

At the Computer

Invite small groups of children to color online. Make sure that every group member has ample time to try the online coloring activity without feeling rushed. Learning how to manipulate a mouse is difficult for young children. After a group of children has colored a picture online, you may wish to print it so it can be displayed in the classroom.

Circle Time

After you have printed some coloring pages, you can add these to your Art or Drawing Center.

What to Say

I have found two interesting ways to color using our computer. The first way is to print pictures that you can color using crayons, markers, or colored pencils. Lots of Web sites on the Internet have cute pictures like the ones you see in coloring books.

The second way to color using our computer is to color online. We are going to try that today. You will use the mouse to pick colors and fill in the pieces of a picture. (Demonstrate how to select a color from the color palette and use that color to fill in a section of the picture.)

Color Palette

Approximate Preparation Time
30 minutes

Learning Concept
This activity increases young children's fine-motor coordination and enhances creativity.

Materials
- white poster board cut into the shape of an art palette, one for each child
- paintbrushes
- poster paints—red, blue, yellow, and white
- small plastic cups

Lesson Preparation
Cut the poster board into the shape of an art palette. Prepare an Art Center with the poster board palettes, poster paint poured into small cups, and paintbrushes.

Directed Teaching Focus
Model this activity by using your palette to show how to mix colors together. Then give children dabs of paint in the primary colors (red, blue, yellow) on their palettes. Have them create the secondary colors by mixing the paints as specified in the box shown below. Mix white into some of the colors on your palette to show how it changes the colors to lighter shades.

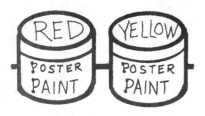

Color Mixing List
red + blue = purple
red + yellow = orange
blue + yellow = green
red + blue + yellow = brown

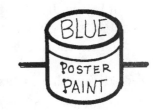

Note: Mix primary and secondary colors together for more colors. Mix white with any of the colors to make different shades.

Self-Directed Activity
Encourage children to continue their exploration of color in the Art Center. If you prefer not to have paints in a self-directed center, children can use chalk, crayons, or markers.

What to Say
I am going to show everyone how to mix the primary colors—red, blue, and yellow—together to make more colors. (Have children name the colors you use and mix.)

Technology Take-Off Point
Decide upon a color of the day for an Internet color search. Use preschool sites that you have bookmarked. To find great preschool sites in a hurry, use **Ask.com** and phrase a question. Then look for a specific color.

Rainbow Colors Gelatin

Approximate Preparation Time

three hours

Learning Concept

This simple cooking activity increases fine-motor coordination, measurement skills, and color recognition skills, and enhances creativity.

Materials

- gelatin (various colors)
- water
- stove or hot plate
- cooking pot
- oven mitts

- measuring cups
- large spoon
- gelatin mold or large glass bowl
- refrigerator

Warnings: Ask parents if their children have any food allergies or dietary restrictions. Never allow children near the stove or hot plate or to handle anything that is hot.

Lesson Preparation

Set up a Cooking Center with the recipe and ingredients for making gelatin. Arrange children's seating so that the lesson can be presented to the whole class or small groups. You may wish to enlist the help of volunteers. Remember to reproduce the recipe for the class cookbook and for student cookbooks that will be sent home at the end of the year. Use crayons to make a picture to show the order of the colored gelatin you will use. If you wish the colors to be in the order of a real rainbow, use this order: red, orange, yellow, green, blue, indigo, and violet.

Directed Teaching Focus

Have children identify the various colors of gelatin by looking at the boxes. Make the gelatin, one color at a time. Pour the gelatin into the mold or glass bowl. Chill that layer until it is firm. Then make the next color gelatin and add that layer on top of the other color. You may only want to use three colors to save time. Allow children to eat the gelatin.

Self-Directed Activity

Let children create rainbows using colored balls in baskets.

What to Say

(If you are making the gelatin at home, describe the process for children. Otherwise, have children help you make the recipe. Be sure they understand that they will have to wait for each layer to be firm before adding the next layer.)

Technology Take-Off Point

Check out the official JELL-O Web site (**http://www.jell-o.com/**) for more fun with gelatin. Here you can learn the history of JELL-O. Read a salute to Bill Cosby, the JELL-O spokesman for over 25 years. Of course, this site is full of fun recipes.

I Can Color!

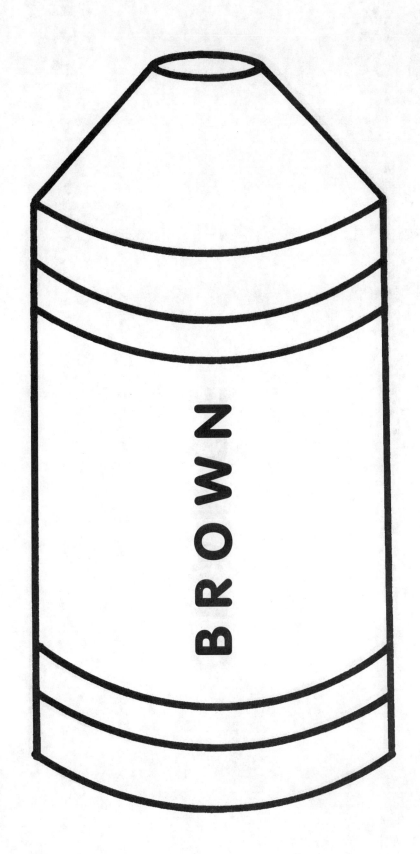

I Can Color! *(cont.)*

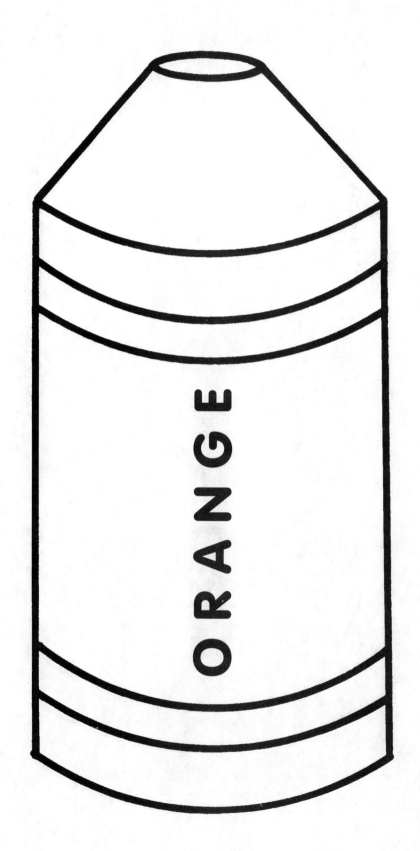

I Can Color! (cont.)

I Can Color! *(cont.)*

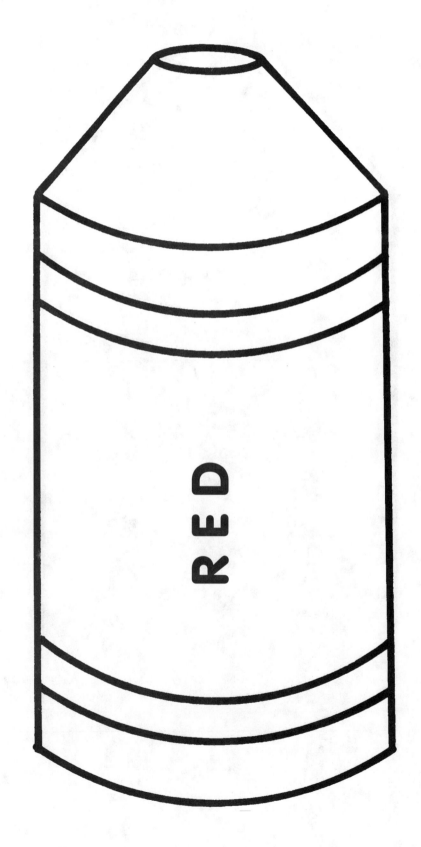

I Can Color! *(cont.)*

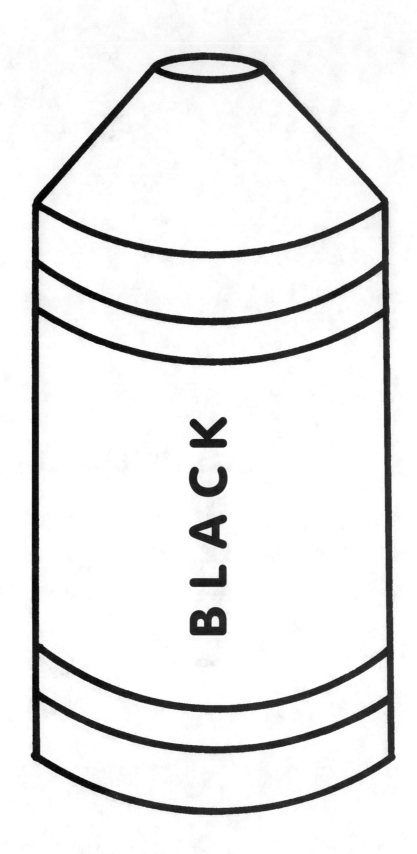

I Can Color! *(cont.)*

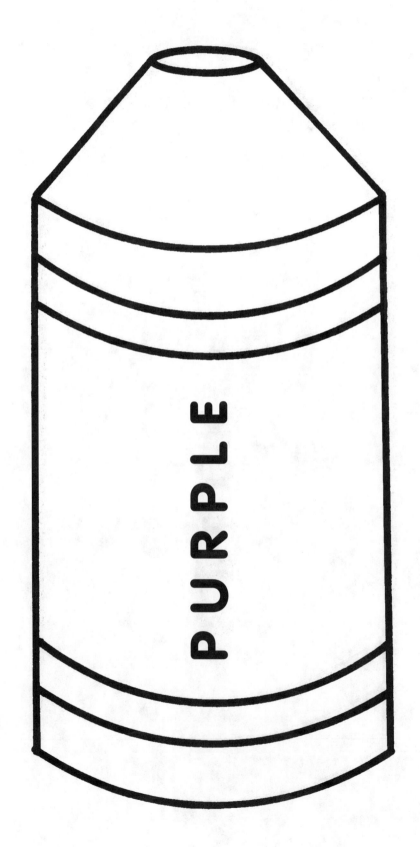

I Can Color! *(cont.)*

I Can Color! *(cont.)*

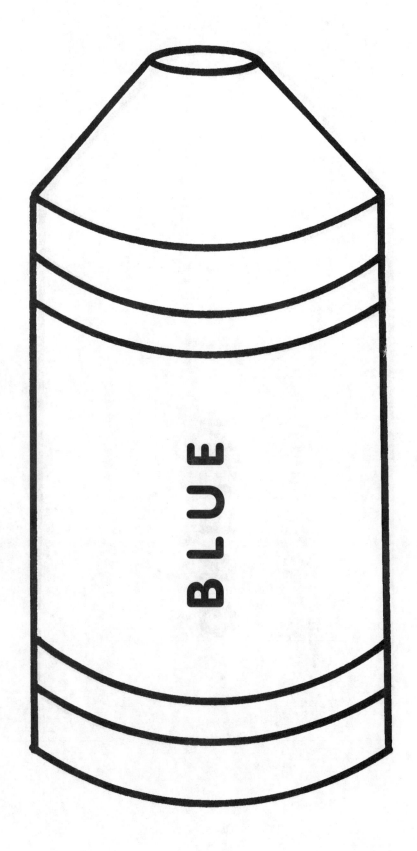

Theater and Puppets

Hands-On Internet Activities

Favorite Star Search

Favorite Star Wallpaper

Thematic Activities

Art—Penguin Puppets

Dramatic Play—Penguin Puppet Show

Storybook—Daisy's Day at the Theater

Annotated Web Sites

Children's Creative Theater

http://tqjunior.advanced.org/5291/

This theater site, designed for children, is an excellent resource for early childhood teachers as you research activity ideas that will help you bring theater into your classrooms in a way that children can enjoy. The site, connected to The Rose Blumkin Performing Arts Center, is "one of the most wonderful children's theaters in the world." The Web site features of photo tour of a real theater. Make sure not to miss the theater games section, which is very well written and has activities for children of different ages.

The Puppetry Home page

http://www.sagecraft.com/puppetry/

This site is written and maintained by Rose Sage, a puppetry expert. It has a variety of information about puppets, the art of puppetry, puppetry events, definitions of various kinds of puppetry, pictures and photos of puppetry and puppets, a description of puppetry traditions around the world, and even a list of questions and answers about puppetry. This is a very comprehensive Web site for you to begin your research about puppets.

Hans Christian Andersen: Fairy Tales and Stories

http://www.math.technion.ac.il/~rl/Andersen/

Fairy tales make excellent dramatic play opportunities in your early childhood classroom. This Web site is an amazing find for anyone interested in the fairy tales of Hans Christian Andersen. Zvi Har'El, a senior lecturer in the Department of Mathematics at the Technion, Israel Institute of Technology, created this interesting site.

Mother Goose Rebus Rhymes

http://www.enchantedlearning.com/Rhymes.html

Take a look at all of these interesting Mother Goose rebus rhymes and see if children can help you "read" them. Children can act out these short rhymes during dramatic play time.

Suggested Keyword Searches

fairy tales, children's literature, children's stories, children's poetry, nursery rhymes, movie stars, heroes, athletes (You may also wish to search for specific story, nursery rhyme, or poetry titles; authors; and movie stars, heroes, and athletes.)

Favorite Star Search

Approximate Preparation Time

two hours

Learning Concept

This activity increases young children's decision-making skills, as well as their understanding of sequence.

Materials

- classroom computer
- bookmarked Web sites
- printer paper (optional)
- Internet Service Provider (ISP)
- printer (optional)

Lesson Preparation

Ahead of time, have children select a favorite hero, athlete, or movie/TV star. Preview and bookmark Web sites that tell about these heroes, athletes, and movie/TV stars. Be sure that all the information and pictures provided at each site is appropriate for young children.

Circle and Center Time

Have children brainstorm a list of athletes, heroes, or movie/TV stars. Then talk with children about their favorite personalities. Ask them to tell why they like a particular athlete, hero, or movie/TV star. Then explain to children that they will get a chance to find out about their favorite personality using the Internet.

At the Computer

Have children access the information that you have bookmarked about their favorite athletes, heroes, or movie/TV stars. Read and discuss the information with the class. Allow children to summarize the information provided on the Web sites.

You may wish to print the pictures of or information about the different personalities for a bulletin board entitled "Our Favorite Famous People."

What to Say

First, I want you to name your favorite _____ (athletes, heroes, or movie stars). I will write the names on the board as you name these people. We are going to find out more about them on the Internet.

Favorite Star Wallpaper

Approximate Preparation Time

one hour

Learning Concept

This activity increases young children's fine-motor coordination, ability to follow directions, and understanding of sequence.

Materials

- classroom computer
- Internet Service Provider (ISP)
- bookmarked Web sites from page 254

Lesson Preparation

Before beginning, go through the steps of creating wallpaper for your computer to make sure you understand how this feature works.

Circle and Center Time

At Circle Time talk with children about their favorite athletes, heroes, or movie/TV stars that they chose in the last activity. Explain to children that they will get to use the picture of their favorite personality to make computer wallpaper. Point out that wallpaper on a computer is the background color, pattern, and/or picture you see on the desktop.

At the Computer

Use the following steps to use a saved image for computer wallpaper.

On a MAC

1. Click Apple, and then click Control Panel.
2. Click Desktop Pictures.
3. Click Select Picture.
4. Click on drop-down listbox to select your image file.
5. Click Desktop. (Notice the picture sample box.)
6. Click Set Desktop. Your wallpaper will appear on your desktop.

On a PC with Windows:

1. Click Start. Drag to Settings, and then Control Panel.
2. Double-click on the Display icon.
3. Click the Background tab at the top.
4. Click the *Browse* button to search for the image saved on your hard drive or disk.
5. Click on the file. Then click OK. Your wallpaper will appear on your desktop.

What to Say

Today we are going to use the pictures of our favorite personalities to make something called computer wallpaper. Wallpaper on a computer is the background color, pattern, and/or picture we see on the desktop. Let me show you what I mean by wallpaper. (Change the wallpaper to different colors and patterns as children watch. Then guide them as they use the pictures of famous people to create wallpaper.)

Penguin Puppets

Approximate Preparation Time

one hour

Learning Concept

This simple activity increases children's ability to follow directions in sequence and improves their fine-motor coordination.

Materials

- classroom computer
- Internet Service Provider (ISP)
- bookmarked Web sites
- Penguin Puppet Pattern (page 258), one for each child
- scissors

- glue
- cardstock
- large craft sticks
- masking tape
- example puppets or pictures of puppets

Lesson Preparation

Preview and bookmark Web sites that tell about puppets and puppetry.

Reproduce the Penguin Puppet Pattern, making one for each child. These puppets are so simple to make that you may wish to consider making the same kind of puppets using different characters for your Dramatic Play Center.

Set up an Art Center with the necessary materials for children to assemble the stick puppets.

Directed Teaching Focus

Introduce this activity by talking about different kinds of puppets. Bring several different kinds of puppets to show children. Consider showing examples of hand puppets, stick puppets, marionettes, sock puppets, and paper bag puppets. If you do not have access to any puppets, show pictures of puppets in books.

Then use the Internet to introduce children to the various kinds of puppets.

Model how to make the stick puppet using the directions on page 257. Help children make their own penguin puppet.

Later use the puppets to put on a puppet show. See pages 259 and 260 for this activity.

Penguin Puppets *(cont.)*

Assemble each puppet using the following steps:

1. Cut out the penguin pattern.

2. Glue the penguin pattern onto a piece of cardstock.

3. After the glue dries, cut out the pattern from the cardstock.

4. Place the pattern face down. Lay one end of a craft stick on the back of the pattern.

5. Secure the craft stick to the back of the puppet using masking tape.

6. Hold the puppet using the unused end of the craft stick.

Self-Directed Activity

After children have completed the penguin puppets, let them try out the puppets in your puppet theatre. If you don't have a puppet theater yet, consider one of the ideas on page 259.

What to Say

I have brought some different kinds of puppets for you to look at. (If you don't have access to any puppets, use books to show pictures of some different kinds.) What kinds of puppets do you have at home? (Ask children to describe any puppets they have at home.) Who has put on a puppet show or been to see a puppet show? (Allow children to share their experiences.) Today we are going to learn about puppets by looking at puppets that I have brought (or those in books and on the Internet). Then we will even make our own puppets.

Technology Take-Off Point

You will find that there are many interesting puppet sites that you can visit to gather puppet information for this unit. See the Annotated Web Sites (page 253) for a site that describes the history of puppets, gives information about various kinds of puppets, and has a variety of interesting links.

Penguin Puppet Pattern

Penguin Puppet Show

Approximate Preparation Time
two hours

Learning Concept
This activity enhances children's dramatic play ability, creativity, listening skills, and their ability to follow directions. In addition, this activity improves youngsters' sequencing skills.

Materials
- Penguin Puppets (page 256–258)
- puppet stage
- Penguin Poem (page 261)
- digital camera or regular camera with film developed to CD-ROM

Lesson Preparation
You will need to make the penguin puppets on pages 256–258 before beginning this puppet show activity.

Reproduce the Penguin Poem for children.

Then create some kind of puppet stage. The stage can be as simple or as complex as you wish. Consider some of the following ideas for the stage:

- Turn a table on its side and have children hold their puppets above the edge from behind the table.
- Have children hide behind a couch or sofa and hold puppets up from behind it.
- Buy a puppet stage at a children's toy or educational store.
- Use a large appliance box (such as those used for refrigerators) and cut out a large window for the puppet stage.
- Have children stand in a row with their puppets and act out the poem without a traditional stage.

Penguin Puppet Show *(cont.)*

Directed Teaching Focus

Introduce this activity by talking to children about puppet shows and the puppets they have made. Explain that you have a penguin poem that you want to read while children use their puppets to act out the parts of the penguins.

Begin by reading the poem aloud and talking about what children might do with their penguin puppets to create a puppet show that goes with the poem. Then divide children into groups of four and read the penguin poem again, have children act out the parts in their own way.

Try it again, designating roles (penguins 1–4) for the children acting out the puppet show. Ask each child to hide her or his penguin when you read the part that describes how that penguin swims away. Practice until children feel comfortable with their roles.

The puppet show requires four puppeteers, so you can repeat the poem again until all children have had a chance to use their puppets and take part in the puppet show.

Self-Directed Activity

After you have a puppet stage in place in your Dramatic Play Center, you will be ready to create different puppets to allow children to express themselves. Consider making animal and people puppets. In addition, you can have children hold up old stuffed animals and dolls to use as puppets.

Consider recording your voice as you read the penguin poem. Then place the tape in the Dramatic Play Center. Let children replay this tape as they act out the poem with their penguin puppets.

You may also wish to record a variety of nursery rhymes or other stories for children to act out using puppets and add these to your Dramatic Play Center.

What to Say

I am going to read you a poem about penguins. After I am done, you will get to have your own puppet show using the penguin puppets you have made. Listen as I read the poem. Then let's talk about how we can act out the poem using the puppets.

Technology Take-Off Point

While children perform their puppet show, take lots of pictures using your digital or regular camera. If you use a regular camera, make sure to get the film developed on CD-ROM so you will be able to view these photos on your computer.

Penguin Poem

by Daisy Jasmine
(Age 7)

Four little penguins
You and I see.
One swam away,
Then there were three.

Three little penguins
Smiling at you.
One swam away,
Then there were two.

Two little penguins
Sitting in the sun.
One swam away,
Then there was one.

One little penguin
Was a hero.
One swam away,
Then there were zero.

Zero little penguins—
There are no more.
We ask them back,
Now there are four!

Daisy's Day at the Theater

Today is a special day for Daisy. She's going to the theater with her mother. It's not the kind of theater that shows movies on a screen. This theater has real people who act on a stage.

Daisy's Day at the Theater *(cont.)*

Daisy has an uncle named Chad. He is a stage actor, not a movie actor. Daisy's mother is taking her to see Uncle Chad act in a stage play.

Daisy's Day at the Theater (cont.)

Daisy and her mother arrive at the theater. Uncle Chad greets them and shows them around. There are many interesting things to see and learn about.

Daisy's Day at the Theater (cont.)

First Uncle Chad shows Daisy and her mother the stage. This is where the actors perform. The seats all around the stage are where the audience sits. The people in audience must be very quiet to hear what the actors say.

Daisy's Day at the Theater *(cont.)*

Uncle Chad shows Daisy the stage sets. Sets are large boards called flats that make the actors look like they are standing in a real place when they are on stage. Uncle Chad stands in front of a set that looks like a beach.

266

Daisy's Day at the Theater *(cont.)*

Daisy meets the stage manager. A stage manager is the person who makes sure everything goes well during the play. A stage manager stands in back of the stage and watches everything. The manager wears a tiny microphone so he or she can talk to the people who work on the lights and the sound.

Daisy's Day at the Theater *(cont.)*

Uncle Chad takes Daisy and her mother to the light booth. The people who sit in the light booth turn the lights on and off and they make the lights turn different colors.

Uncle Chad lets Daisy push a button. A bright blue light shines on the stage.

Daisy's Day at the Theater (cont.)

It's time for the actors to get ready. Daisy and her mother watch the costumer help Uncle Chad put on his costume. The costumer makes all the clothes that the actors wear.

Daisy's Day at the Theater *(cont.)*

Then a make-up artist puts stage makeup on Uncle Chad's face. This way the audience will be able to clearly see his face when he is on stage.

Daisy's Day at the Theater (cont.)

When Uncle Chad is ready to go on stage, he talks to the director. The director tells the actors what to do on stage. Uncle Chad and the other actors will perform the play.

Daisy's Day at the Theater (cont.)

It is almost time for the play to begin. Daisy kisses Uncle Chad and says, "Break a leg." This is the way people in the theater say, "Good luck!"

Daisy's Day at the Theater *(cont.)*

Daisy and her mother sit in the audience. The curtains open and the play begins. Daisy and her mother sit quietly as they watch the play. They want to hear all the actors.

When the play is over, the audience claps loudly. Daisy and her mother clap loudly, too. Then Daisy and her mother go backstage to hug Uncle Chad and tell him he did a great job.

Daisy's Day at the Theater (cont.)

Daisy had a wonderful time at the theater.

Selecting an Internet Service Provider

Activity

The first thing you need to do in order to use the Internet, is select an Internet Service Provider (ISP). An ISP is the service through which you gain access to the Internet and all of its features—the World Wide Web, e-mail, mailing lists, newsgroups, and real-time chat environments.

There are many ISPs. You can choose a large company, like America Online, or you can choose a smaller company that might be a local business. Whichever ISP you choose, you will want to carefully consider what the ISP has to offer and how that fits into your plans for using the Internet in your classroom.

The ISP you select will also depend on whether you are using a PC or a MAC. Unfortunately for MAC users, there are far fewer options because the ISP's software is often not compatible with the MAC operating system. However, MAC users still have a number of excellent choices.

Materials

- classroom computer
- Internet Service Provider (ISP)

Directions

Getting information about an ISP can be accomplished several ways. Choose one of these methods:

- Log on to the Internet at your local library and peruse the home pages of the ISPs that you are considering. Print information that is relevant and make your decision. After you have made your choice, you will need to obtain ISP software to install on your classroom computer to begin.
- You can use free software samples that you receive in computer magazines or by calling the ISP and requesting that the software be sent to you. Then sign up for a trial membership, consisting of free hours, to try the service and see if it meets your needs.
- Ask your friends and other teachers about the ISPs that they use.

Selecting an Internet Service Provider *(cont.)*

Once you have selected an ISP and you have the necessary software to install it, use these basic directions. Your directions may vary slightly depending on the software you choose. In most cases, it will be extremely easy to click your way through the information needed to sign up and log on.

1. Place the CD-ROM or disk in the appropriate drive of your computer. Click Start. For a PC, drag to Run and then Open. In most computers using Windows 95 or better, your computer will automatically recognize and begin installation of the software. Otherwise, in the Open textbox type the letter of the drive that the software is in. Then click OK.

   If you are using a MAC, insert the CD-ROM or disk in the appropriate drive of your computer. Double-click on the software's icon on your desktop. Sometimes the software installation will automatically begin. However, in most cases you will need to double-click the icon to open the disk or CD-ROM. Then locate the installer icon. Double-click on the installer icon and installation will begin.

2. Follow the software's installation directions. Remember, at this point you will need to have a modem and an active phone line plugged into your computer.

3. Have your credit card ready to enter credit information. Make a note of the type of services you are choosing. Keep a written record of the following things:

   - Free hours—Many ISPs offer a free hours on a trial basis.
   - Trial period—Make a note of when this period starts and ends in case you decide to change to a different ISP.
   - Your password—This is the secret word or code that you use to log on. Be sure to write it down and keep it in a safe place.
   - Your screen name—This is your short on-screen name and is most likely the beginning of your e-mail address.
   - Your e-mail address—When you sign up and selecting your on-screen name you will also be given your complete e-mail address. Jot this down. It should look something like this example: yourname@ISPname.com.

Technology Take-Off Point

Below are a couple of large ISPs. You may wish to begin in your search with one of these.

America Online (AOL)
1-888-235-0890
http://www.aol.com

Microsoft Network (MSN)
1-800-386-5550
http://www.msn.com

Free Internet Service Providers

Activity

Many Internet Services Providers (ISPs) offer unlimited usage for a set monthly fee. This makes the Internet accessible to practically anyone who owns a computer. However, some free Internet Service Providers (ISPs) are also available. If you are willing to weed through the advertising they display on their site, you can use the Internet in your classroom for free. Use the directions provided below to set up a free ISP called NetZero.

Note: NetZero currently supports Windows 95, Windows 98, and NT. They are planning a MAC version, and by clicking on the *Requirements* button on the Join NetZero page you can access an e-mail address that invites you to send e-mail that expresses your interest in a MAC version of the software.

Materials

- classroom computer
- Internet Service Provider (ISP)
- Windows 95 or better or NT
- five blank 3.5" floppy disks (optional)

Directions
How to sign up for NetZero

Method 1: Use an existing e-mail account to send a letter to free4anyone@netzero.net requesting a CD-ROM with all the files you need. When it arrives, follow the instructions to load it onto your computer. The directions should match closely to the steps provided on page 278 for online access.

Method 2: Using Internet accesses provided by an existing account with another ISP, log onto the following Web site:

http://www.netzero.net/main.html

<Figure 1-1> NetZero home page

Free Internet Service Providers *(cont.)*

The NetZero home page has information that you can read to find out how the service works and get most of your questions answered before you dive in. Look around a bit, then click the *Join NetZero* button. This will take you to a new screen with more information about NetZero membership. Choose the *Download Click Here* button.

<Figure 1-2> NetZero software download options

Now you are presented with different options on how to download the NetZero software for the machine you will use to access the Internet. See Figure 1-2.

1. If you are already on the machine that you will normally use to connect to the Internet, choose the Full Download option. If you plan to connect to the Internet from a different machine, you will need five blank IBM formatted floppy disks so you can make a copy of the software. Later you can use the disks to install the software on the machine you will use. Choose the Diskette Download option if that is appropriate.

2. Either option you choose will send you to a page that shows the NetZero User Agreement. If you do not accept the agreement, then you cannot go any further.

3. If you accept the agreement you will see a screen with detailed instructions on how to download NetZero software according to the option you chose. Follow the step-by-step instructions provided.

4. After following either set of instructions, you eventually end up with a file on your computer called netzero.exe. Double-click on that file in the Windows Explorer program to start the program. NetZero assumes you already have a web browser installed on your machine. Almost every Windows 95 or better PC comes with the Microsoft Internet Explorer browser pre-installed. This will work fine. If you have another browser such as Netscape Navigator, that works well, too.

   Note: The America Online browser only works while you are connected to the Internet using their service. The AOL browser is not compatible with NetZero.

5. A NetZero setup program will run on your machine. It will prompt you to confirm agreement to the NetZero User Agreement and Terms and Conditions for Use. It will create a directory on your computer to store its own files and set up an icon on your desktop. Just before it is finished, choose the launch NetZero option box.

Free Internet Service Providers *(cont.)*

6. The NetZero Logon window has a button to create new accounts. Select that button now.

7. Agree to the screens about preventing fraud and the NetZero Terms and Conditions.

8. Choose an identifier for your NetZero account. It will be part of your NetZero e-mail address, so choose carefully. The screen provides all the rules for creating an acceptable name. Choose Next.

9. Choose a password and confirm it. Again there are a number of guidelines posted to help you create a good password. Choose Next.

10. In case you ever forget your password, or need to prove that you are the owner of that account, NetZero provides you with a form to fill out. On this form you give a question and the answer. (If you forget your password, NetZero will ask you your question and you will have to type in the pre-arranged answer.) Choose Next.

11. Identify if your primary purpose for using the Internet is business or personal. Also confirm that you are over 18 years of age since minors cannot have NetZero accounts.

<Figure 1-3> Choose the NetZero dial-up number.

12. Choose a phone number to access the Internet using NetZero. Select your telephone area code or state, a nearby city, a phone number, and dialing options from a series of menus. Choose Next. Confirm your readiness to have your computer dial-up NetZero and start surfing the Web.

Free Internet Service Providers *(cont.)*

If you chose a user name that someone else has already chosen, you will be prompted to select another until you pick one that is unique. If your user name does not match one already in existence and you don't have any problems with your modem or your computer, you will be connected to NetZero. NetZero will automatically start your browser and open up to the NetZero home page. You are now connected to the Internet for free.

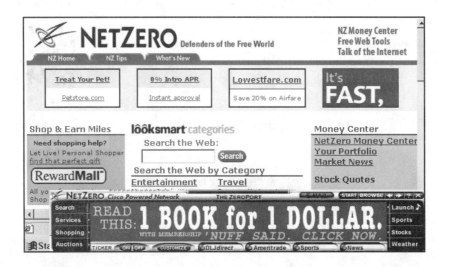

<Figure 1-4> NetZero home page means you are successfully connected.

Now you will see the NetZero ZeroPort appear on your screen. This is the way this delivers the advertising to you while you use the ISP. It has many features and customizing options you will want to explore. You may need to move it to see parts of your screen. To do so, use your mouse to grab the ZeroPort on the top middle and drag it to a different location. Remember that if you hide or close the ZeroPort, your Internet access is disconnected.

Technology Take-Off Point

NetZero is only one of a growing number of free full-feature ISPs available to you. You should spend some time looking at several different ISPs before selecting one. Check out the Web sites. You may wish to try each of them. A couple of free access companies which compare to NetZero are FreeI.Net (**http://www.freei.net/**) and AltaVista FreeAccess (**http://microav.com/**). A comprehensive list of over 4,000 ISPs with descriptions is available at the following Web site:

http://www.isps.com/

Microsoft Internet Explorer–Searches and Bookmarks

Activity

A browser is your Internet surfboard. Almost every PC computer has a copy of Microsoft Internet Explorer preloaded if it has Windows 95 or better. MAC users can also use Internet Explorer and in some of the more recent systems and with Microsoft Office it comes preloaded. If you do not already have Microsoft Internet Explorer and you wish to download it, go to Microsoft Internet Explorer home page:

http://www.microsoft.com/windows/ie/

Most browsers are very similar because they are designed to help you do the same thing—surf the Net. In this activity, you will learn how to use the Microsoft Internet Explorer toolbar, how to search for something on the Internet, how to bookmark Web sites, and how to use the Favorites feature.

Materials

- classroom computer
- Internet Service Provider (ISP)
- Microsoft Internet Explorer

Directions

Begin by logging onto your ISP. If your ISP does not automatically open Internet Explorer, you will have to open it yourself. If you are using a PC, find it by clicking Start. Drag to Programs and then Internet Explorer. If you are using a MAC, click the Internet Explorer alias on your desktop or in your Launcher or locate Internet Explorer by clicking the Apple icon on the toolbar. If you are a MAC user and you are not familiar with the Internet Explorer icon or alias, see Figure 2-1.

<Figure 2-1> Internet Explorer icon or alias

Maximize your browser window to help you see everything you need in order to understand and follow along with this activity. You can maximize any window by double-clicking on the colored bar across the top of that window or by clicking once on the little box that appears in the colored bar in the top right-hand corner. MAC users can click on the bottom right-hand corner and drag it to enlarge the window.

Microsoft Internet Explorer–Searches and Bookmarks *(cont.)*

When you open your browser, the Internet Explorer home page appears as shown in Figure 2-2.

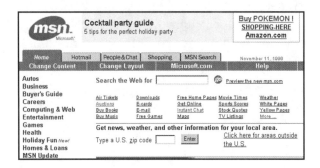

<Figure 2-2> Internet Explorer home page

This is the Internet Explorer default setting, but you can change it to open with any home page you want. Directions for how to do this are given in the description of the Home button on page 283.

<Figure 2-3> Internet Explorer browser toolbar

Now take a look at the Internet Explorer browser toolbar as pictured in Figure 2-3. As you read each of the following descriptions (pages 282–284), look at the figure and find the button shown on the toolbar. Then find the corresponding button on your toolbar on the screen.

Toolbar Functions

Back—This button allows you to go back to the page or window you were viewing just before. You can click on this more than once to return to previous pages or windows. By choosing the down arrow adjacent to the Back button you can see a list of previously viewed Web pages and jump directly to the page you like.

Forward—This button allows you to move forward. You can only go forward after you have already gone back at least once.

Stop—This button allows you to stop loading the Web site you are trying to access. This is particularly helpful for sites that take too long to load or if you change your mind and decide to go to a different site.

Microsoft Internet Explorer–Searches and Bookmarks *(cont.)*

Locate the buttons described below in Figure 2-3 (page 282).

Refresh—This button allows you to reload the Web page you are currently viewing. This is especially useful if you encounter any problems or hang-ups in getting a Web site to display correctly.

Home—This button loads your home page. Internet Explorer users usually default to **http://www.msn.com/** or the home page established by your Internet Service Provider. If you find another site that you prefer for your home page, there is an easy way to change your default setting. First navigate to the page you want by typing in the Web site address in the Address textbox. Then click on Tools. Drag to Internet Options, General, and then Use Current. Afterwards, clicking the *Home* button will return you to your new home page.

Address Textbox—This textbox is the space in which you type the Web site address, or URL, you are interested in visiting on the World Wide Web. The adjacent down arrow will reveal a shortcut history to other Web addresses that you have recently visited.

Go—This button allows you to go to the address you have typed in the Address textbox.

Search—This button accesses the Internet Explorer Search textbox that allows you to search the Internet using keywords. You can tailor features of this utility by choosing the Customize button from this screen. Click the *Search* button and your screen will change as shown in Figure 2-4. Then click the *Customize* button, which is now available and the screen changes again, allowing you to make alterations to the way you search as shown in Figures 2-4 and 2-5.

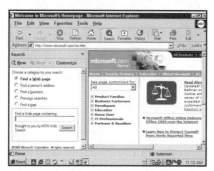

<Figure 2-4> Clicking the Search button changes the screen.

<Figure 2-5> The Internet Explorer customize search setting dialog box appears when you click the Customize button.

Microsoft Internet Explorer–Searches and Bookmarks *(cont.)*

Now take a moment to return to the toolbar. Locate the buttons described below in Figure 2-3 (page 282).

Favorites—This button helps you keep track of Web sites that you want to remember and be able to quickly revisit. Click it when you want to save a site that you like. Notice when you click *Favorites* your browser screen splits and you will see your list of favorites on the left. Click the *Add* button and then click OK to add the Web page currently showing in your browser screen to your list of favorites.

History—This button lets you review all the sites you have visited in the last few days. You can change the number of days available by clicking Tools, and then Internet Options, and then General, and then History.

Mail—This button launches your e-mail program. It will automatically choose whatever your default e-mail program is. If you want to change the e-mail program selected, click the Mail button, click Tools, Internet Options, Programs, and then E-mail. You will see a drop-down listbox that allows you to change the e-mail settings.

Print—This button sends the page you are viewing to your printer. You can change the default settings for your printer by clicking File and then Print. The Print dialog box will appear.

Doing a Search

Now that you have a basic overview of Microsoft Internet Explorer browser toolbar, you are ready to conduct a search.

1. Click the *Search* button.
2. In the Search textbox, write a word or words that reflects the topic, such as preschool activities, that you wish to find information about on the World Wide Web. Click the *Search* button.

<Figure 2-6> Internet Explorer search window after a search

This search will produce results that contain either word or both words. Consequently, you will see a number of Web sites that have nothing to do with the topic you want. In order to get only results for both words together, enclose them in quotes—"preschool activities." This makes the words a phrase and the Web sites you receive from your search will contain the whole phrase "preschool activities." This type of search should produce more accurate results.

Microsoft Internet Explorer–Searches and Bookmarks *(cont.)*

Creating a Web Site Bookmark

1. Click on the first three search results and review them quickly.

2. Using the Back and Forward buttons, return to a site that you wish to make one of your favorites.

3. Bookmark this page by clicking the Favorites button. In the Favorites dialog box, click Add. Notice that the left side of your browser has now changed from the search options area to your Favorites list. A special Add Favorite dialog box will appear.

4. If you choose the OK box to save the site to your Favorites list right now, Internet Explorer will save the address for you to find at some future time but you must be connected to the Internet. However, you may wish to bookmark sites so they are available to your class at a future time without being connected to the Internet. To do so, click the box marked Make Available Offline. Another program called Wizard will walk you through a few questions to allow you to select your preferences. One of the important questions you will need to consider is whether or not you want to store all the other pages that are linked to the page you are viewing. Be sure to carefully review all linked pages before you choose to store them on your classroom computer.

5. Finally, click OK to bookmark your favorite page.

Technology Take-Off Point

The ability to bookmark your favorite pages so that you can use them even when you are offline can make your classroom computer a safe and exciting place for preschoolers to have enriching experiences with Internet. Using the Internet offline avoids the problems of tying up a telephone line, waiting for slow pages to load, or accidentally exposing students to inappropriate material that can be found on the Internet.

Netscape Navigator–Searches and Bookmarks

Activity

Netscape was one of the first commercially successful browsers for the Internet. Netscape has versions that work on MACs and with Windows for PCs. It offers a whole suite of Internet user tools called Communicator. The browser piece of that suite is called Netscape Navigator. Just like Microsoft Internet Explorer, Netscape Navigator is available for download from the Internet. If you would like a copy on your machine, download it from the Netscape home page:

http://home.netscape.com

No matter which ISP you use to connect to the Internet, you can still use Netscape Navigator as your browser.

In this activity you will learn how to use the Netscape Navigator toolbar, how to search for something on the Internet, how to bookmark Web sites, and how to use the Favorites feature.

Materials

- classroom computer
- Internet Service Provider (ISP)
- Netscape Navigator

Directions

Begin by logging onto your ISP. Launch the Netscape Navigator browser. It may be available as an icon on the Windows desktop or on the small icon tray on your Windows taskbar. It should be available as an alias on the MAC. If you don't find it on a PC, click Start, drag to Programs, then Netscape Communicator, and then Netscape Navigator. For a MAC, click the Apple and look for the program by first clicking the alias on your desktop, and then clicking on Applications or Internet folder.

You can maximize any window by double-clicking on the colored bar across the top of that window or by clicking once on the little box that appears in the colored bar in the top right-hand corner. MAC users can click on the bottom right hand corner and drag it to enlarge the window.

The first thing you see when you open Netscape is called your home page. You can change your home page to something else any time you wish. Directions for how to do this are given in the description of the *Home* button provided on page 287.

Now take a look at the Netscape Navigator browser toolbar as pictured in Figure 3-1 (page 287). As you read each of the following descriptions (pages 287 and 288), look at the figure and find the button shown on the toolbar. Then find the corresponding button on your toolbar on the screen.

Netscape Navigator–Searches and Bookmarks *(cont.)*

<Figure 3-1> Netscape Navigator browser toolbar

Toolbar Functions

Back—This button allows you to go back to the page or window you were viewing just before. You can click on this more than once to return to previous pages or windows. By choosing the down arrow adjacent to the Back button you can see a list of previously viewed Web pages and jump directly to the page you like.

Forward—This button allows you to move forward. You can only go forward after you have already gone back at least once.

Stop—This button allows you to stop loading the Web site you are trying to access. This is particularly helpful for sites that take too long to load or if you change your mind and decide to go to a different site.

Reload—This button allows you to reload the Web page you are currently viewing. This is especially useful if you encounter any problems or hang-ups in getting a Web site to display correctly.

Home—This button loads your home page. Netscape Navigator users usually default to **http://home.netscape.com** or the home page established by your Internet Service Provider. If you ever find another site you prefer for your home page, there is an easy way you can change your default setting. First navigate to the page you want by typing in the Web site address in the Address textbox. Choose Edit and then Preferences as shown in Figure 3-2. Then select Category: Navigator, then Home page, and then Use Current Page. Afterwards, clicking the *Home* button will return you to your new home page.

<Figure 3-2> The Preferences: Navigator dialog box

Netscape Navigator–Searches and Bookmarks *(cont.)*

Locate the buttons described below in Figure 3-1 (page 287).

Search—This button sends you to a Web page operated by the Netscape company at **http://search.netscape.com/** as shown in Figure 3-3.

<Figure 3-3> Netscape Navigator default search page

My Netscape—This sends you to a personal start page. In this case it is a service provided by the Netscape Company allowing you to tailor a range of features and services for your convenience. It is designed so computer novices can walk through a list of choices and get something they would like to see every time they use the Internet. Play with it to see if it is for you. Even if you don't use Netscape Navigator you can access this utility at the following Web site:

http://my.netscape.com/

Print—This button sends the page you are viewing to your printer. If you are looking at a page broken into "frames," click on the frame you want to print before clicking the Print button. You can change the default settings for your printer by clicking File and then Print. The Print dialog box will appear.

Security—This has to do with using your credit card and trusting sites with private personal data. You may never need to use this button.

Netsite Textbox—This textbox is the space in which you type the Web site address, or URL, you are interested in visiting on the World Wide Web. The adjacent down arrow will reveal a shortcut history to other recently typed web addresses. Press the Enter key to go to that address.

Bookmarks—This button allows you to add, edit, or return to an Internet Web site.

Your Personal Toolbar—This toolbar is created by you when you save bookmarks using Bookmarks, File Bookmark, and then Personal. It is a very handy bookmark list.

What's Related—This button gives you hints as to other relevant places to go to get similar or associated information. Don't forget this button when you are surfing the Web and have not found exactly what you are looking for.

Netscape Navigator–Searches and Bookmarks *(cont.)*

Doing a Search

Now that you have a basic overview of Netscape Navigator browser toolbar, you are ready to conduct a search. There are many great search engines on the Internet. Search engine sites can make great home pages.

1. Click the *Search* button.
2. In the Search textbox, write a word or words that reflects the topic, such as preschool activities, that you wish to find information about on the World Wide Web. Click the *Search* button or *Go* or *Go To It*.

This search will produce results that contain either word or both words. Consequently, you will see a number of Web sites that have nothing to do with the topic you want. In order to get only results for both words together, enclose them in quotes—"preschool activities." This makes the words a phrase and the Web sites you receive from your search will contain the whole phrase "preschool activities." This type of search should produce more accurate results as shown in Figure 3-4.

<Figure 3-4> Navigator search results window

Notice that if you choose the Search Tips hyperlink, you can get more help in narrowing down your results to a manageable number. The tips vary with the search utility.

Creating a Web Site Bookmark

1. Click on the first three search results and review them quickly.
2. Using the *Back* and *Forward* buttons, return to a site that you wish to make one of your favorites.
3. Bookmark this page by clicking the *Bookmarks* button.

Netscape Navigator–Searches and Bookmarks *(cont.)*

4. In the Bookmarks dialog box choose Add Bookmark as shown in Figure 3-5.

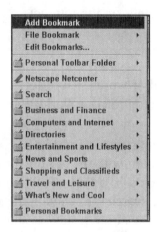

<Figure 3-5> Navigator bookmarks menu

5. Add the Web site to your personal toolbar by choosing Bookmarks, File Bookmark, then Personal.

6. If you choose the OK box to save the site to your Favorites list right now, Netscape Navigator will save the address for you to find at some future time but you must be connected to the Internet. However, you may wish to bookmark sites so they are available to your class at a future time without being connected to the Internet. As long as that page and all its attached files are still stored in your Netscape Cache directory on your PC hard drive, you are able to go back to that page at any time by using your bookmark link. But there is no way to control how long your files will stay in that directory. As you continue to use the Internet, more pages and files get stored there, too. Even if you never bookmark them. Be sure to carefully review all linked pages before you choose to store them on your classroom computer.

Your computer has a set amount of file space it can give to storing Internet data. Eventually older files are pushed out of your Netscape Cache directory—even if you have bookmarked them. Once they are out of your directory, it is impossible to view them offline. Therefore, whenever you plan to use some bookmarked pages while offline, you should be sure to visit those pages while online a day or two before. This will ensure that those pages are updated and ready to use with your class when you need them.

Technology Take-Off Point

The ability to bookmark your favorite pages so that you can use them even when you are offline can make your classroom computer a safe and exciting place for preschoolers to have enriching experiences with Internet. Using the Internet offline avoids the problems of tying up a telephone line, waiting for slow pages to load, or accidentally exposing students to inappropriate material that can be found on the Internet.

Search Engines

Activity

Search engines are software that allow you to search the Internet for specific information. There are many search engines. These are divided into three categories. You will notice that there are pluses and minuses for each category.

Search Engines: This software automatically builds a catalog of Web sites in response to your search. A search engine bases its search on specific criteria that is preprogrammed into the software. It is not a smart search in which a human decides if the results make sense. This is why it is important to learn how to search in a manner that allows you to receive the best and most appropriate responses. Search engines scan the Web to add more information to their catalog, so the results for a search can change on a daily basis.

Directories: These are search tools that have the human touch. A search directory is a catalog of sites that is a hierarchical index. This means that a human decides what makes sense and because of this the list of Web sites you receive in response to a search might make more sense. However, because a directory needs a person to organize the catalogs, the information presented is not as up-to-date as a search engine.

Multi-Threaded Search Engines: These combine several or many search engines together to create a search for you. This can be a very interesting way to search as you usually get more relevant sites than either of the other two methods. A multi-threaded or multi-engine search engine can be an excellent way to search the Web in a more comprehensive manner.

Using the Internet to search for information is something that you will get better at the more you do it. It is important to try a number of different types of search engines and compare the results. In this activity, you will try the same search using several different search engines so you can compare and contrast the results.

Materials

- classroom computer
- Internet Service Provider (ISP)

Directions

For this exercise you will compare WebCrawler, Yahoo!, and Ask.com. You may wish to experiment with other search engines when you have time.

WebCrawler—Search Engine

WebCrawler is a search engine that bases its search results on preprogrammed keywords. When using a standard search engine, it is important to learn how to search effectively. Try to pick specific words that reflect the exact meaning of what you are looking for and do not use extra words. Whenever possible, look for the help feature and read the directions for the search engine you are using. These features give you helpful information about how to conduct a search.

Search Engines *(cont.)*

The help feature of WebCrawler suggests that while you can use plain English searches, you should be specific. Type real language phrases like: *preschools in southern California,* and use the words "not" and "or" in an actual search such as: *Beehives NOT hair* to pinpoint specifics. Use quotes for even more specific searches, such as "Michael Jordan," to make sure you do not get search results for other people named Michael.

1. Log onto your ISP.
2. Enter the URL for WebCrawler (**http://webcrawler.com**) in your browser's Address textbox, and click Go.
3. When the WebCrawler home page appears, type the words "preschool activities" (within quotation marks) in the search textbox.
4. Click Search.
5. Take a look at your results as shown in Figure 4-1, and bookmark your favorites.

<Figure 4-1> WebCrawler home page with your search entered

Yahoo!—Directory Search Engine

Yahoo! is one of the most widely used search engines on the Internet. Besides the regular search engine, which you will use in this, it also has a screened search engine called Yahooligans (**http://www.yahooligans.com/**), which is designed especially for children.

1. Enter the URL for Yahoo (**http://www.yahoo.com/**) in the Address textbox, and click Go. The Yahoo search engine home page will appear as shown in Figure 4-2.

<Figure 4-2> Yahoo search engine home page

Search Engines *(cont.)*

2. Notice you can search using a keyword in the search textbox, or you can click the various categories provided on the page.

3. Type the words "preschool activities" (within quotation marks) in the search textbox.

4. Click Search.

5. Check your results. Click on several sites and take a moment to look at them. Bookmark any sites you are interested in keeping.

Ask Jeeves—Multi-threaded Search Engine

Ask Jeeves is an example of an easy-to-use multi-threaded search engine. All you have to do is frame your search in a question. Then the Ask Jeeves search engine returns your results from a number of other search engines. You can simply click on the sites you want to see.

1. Enter the URL address for Ask Jeeves (**http://www.ask.com**) in the Address textbox, and click Go. The Ask Jeeves search engine home page will appear as shown in Figure 4-3.

<Figure 4-3> Ask Jeeves search engine

2. In the textbox labeled "Just type a question and click 'Ask!' " enter the question, "Where can I find preschool activities?"

3. Then click Ask!

4. You will notice that your search results are returned from a variety of search engines (About.com, WebCrawler, Infoseek, Excite, and AltaVista). Use your mouse to scroll down the page and click on the drop-down listboxes for each search engine's individual results.

5. Now take some time to review the various results from your search. Remember to bookmark your favorite sites.

Technology Take-off Point

There are other multi-engine search engines that can be accessed directly on the Internet, without downloading additional software onto your computer. The Ask Jeeves site (**http://www.ask.com**) provides a variety of links to many other search engines.

E-mail

Activity

E-mail is probably one of the most useful features of the Internet. These days most people have had some exposure to e-mail. E-mail provides a easy way for people to stay in touch with each other—whether they are close by or far apart.

E-mail Services

Because e-mail has become common and is so useful, it makes an excellent in-class tool for use in your early childhood classroom. Almost all e-mail services operate using the same basics. In each one you have an account, an e-mail address, and an electronic form you use to write and send letters. All you have to do is sign up for an e-mail account; ask friends, relatives, and colleagues what their e-mail addresses are; then write and send e-mail.

How do I get an e-mail account?

Almost every Internet Service Provider (ISP), with very few exceptions, includes e-mail services. Even free ISPs include e-mail. In addition, there are many free Internet e-mail services that you can choose regardless of the ISP you have. If you cannot find the e-mail service on your computer, check with the customer help department of your ISP.

Where can I find an e-mail service that is not connected to my ISP?

Finding an e-mail service that is not connected to your ISP is as simple as searching the Internet. Take a look at the Hotmail activity (pages 297–300) to learn about installing and using one of many free Web-based e-mail services.

What do all those letters mean?

If you are using the e-mail service provided by your ISP, you will most frequently use your screen name as the beginning portion of your e-mail address. An e-mail address has a user name, an @ symbol, the company or provider name, a period, and then the organization type. Look at the this example: username@ISPname.com

The organization types, abbreviated by the three letters that appear at the end of each address, include the following:

> **com**—commercial organization
>
> **edu**—educational organization or institution
>
> **net**—network resource organization
>
> **mil**—military organization
>
> **gov**—government organization
>
> **org**—other organizations, including not-for-profit

E-mail *(cont.)*

In this activity you will learn how to write and send e-mail. The example figures provided are from AOL's e-mail program for Windows on a PC. Your e-mail service may look different. However, these examples are provided to give you a general overview of how e-mail works.

Materials

- classroom computer
- Internet Service Provider (ISP)
- e-mail account
- e-mail address of one family member, friend, or colleague (optional)

Directions

Writing E-mail

1. Log onto your e-mail account. This might be through your ISP or another e-mail service.
2. Click on the Mail Center icon, or find the toolbar or menu function that allows you to write or compose an e-mail. Figure 5-1 provides an example dialog box for e-mail.

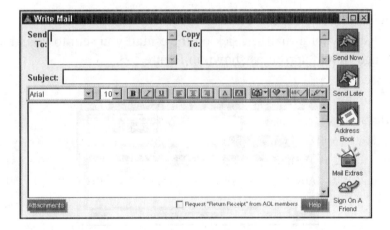

\<Figure 5-1\> AOL Write Mail dialog box

3. Find the place to enter the e-mail address of the person to whom you are sending the e-mail. In the case of AOL, it is called the Send To textbox. Simply type the recipient's e-mail address in this box.
4. Next in the Subject textbox, type the subject as Letter. In the Message textbox or in the place where the body of the letter goes, write your e-mail message.

E-mail *(cont.)*

5. Type a letter something like the one shown in Figure 5-2. Then press the *Send* button to send the e-mail.

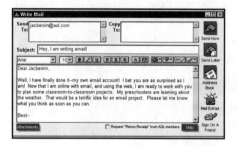

<Figure 5-2> E-mail is not hard to use.

Note: Here is a little trick that you can use to see if your e-mail is working correctly. Try the process again, but in the "send to" space type your own e-mail address. After you send it, you will be able to open and read your own e-mail.

Opening E-mail

Remember that the figures provided as examples might not match the e-mail service you subscribe to.

1. Find the menu item or icon that says "read mail." Click it.

2. You should see a list of your e-mails. Click on the e-mail you sent to yourself and click "read." Your e-mail message should appear as shown in Figure 5-3.

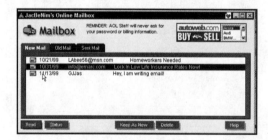

<Figure 5-3> Mail in the mailbox that is ready to be read.

3. Most e-mail forms have a *Reply* button. This button opens a form with the address of the person who sent you the e-mail already placed in the "send to" section.

4. After you read an e-mail you can save or delete it. Locate these features for your own e-mail service.

Technology Take-Off Point

Most e-mail programs now have spell check, which can make a big difference in the quality of the correspondence you send. Remember to use the spell check and to show children how to use it. In addition, most e-mail programs have an address book. This is helpful because it lets you store the e-mail addresses that you want to keep. It is easier to learn to use this feature than to spend time hunting for and typing e-mail addresses.

Free Web-Based Electronic Mail

Activity

As you are probably realizing, e-mail is one of the most useful features of the Internet. The ability to send a message to any place around the globe in just seconds has led to the coining of the term *snail mail* to refer to traditional letters delivered by postal employees.

Most ISPs provide e-mail as part of their services. However, recent developments in Internet technology have given birth to a variety of free Web-based electronic mail services. Web-based e-mail requires a way to access the Internet, which is an ISP, and a browser, which should already be installed on your computer. Most free e-mail services have most or all of the same features as the e-mail services that charge a fee.

Your students' parents may have access to e-mail. If so, e-mail can provide you with an additional means of communication with parents and allow children to share the school experiences with their families.

In this activity, you will learn how to sign up with Microsoft Hotmail, a major free e-mail service provider. In addition, you will see how to get your own e-mail address and be able to send an e-mail message.

Materials

- classroom computer
- Internet Service Provider (ISP)
- e-mail address of one family member, friend, or colleague (optional)

Directions

Signing Up for Microsoft Hotmail

1. Begin by logging onto your ISP. Start your Internet browser.
2. Go to Hotmail by typing in the following address:

   http://www.hotmail.com

3. Click on the *Sign up now!* hyperlink. The Hotmail home page should appear as shown in Figure 6-1.

<Figure 6-1> Hotmail home page

Free Web-Based Electronic Mail *(cont.)*

4. Read and approve the Terms of Service Agreement. Click the I Accept button at the bottom of the screen.

5. Complete the profile information to tell about yourself.

6. Select a name for your e-mail address. In this example, the name "sleepymommy" is used. This will allow Hotmail to create the Internet e-mail address "sleepymommy." Hotmail address names must begin with a letter. The rest of the address can use letters (a–z), numbers (0–9), and the underscore (_). Do not use any spaces within your e-mail address name. Be sure you use a name that is easy to remember.

7. Choose a password. Your e-mail account has to be password protected to preserve your privacy. At Hotmail, passwords must be at least eight characters long. They can contain upper and lowercase letters of the alphabet and/or numbers (0–9). Passwords cannot contain any spaces. Pick a password that is easy for you to remember but hard for others to guess. Be sure to write down your password and put it in a safe place.

8. Enter a secret question and the answer to that question. This question and answer is used in case you ever forget your password and need to prove that you are the owner of the e-mail account. Choose questions with answers that will not change over time and that no one posing as you is likely to guess. You must choose a question and answer that does not use your exact password.

9. Click the *Sign Up* button.

10. Now you will have a chance to get a passport. You will need to type your password again. This passport will give you access to a variety of MSN sites on the Internet. Fill in the information and continue.

11. The next screen should confirm that you have successfully signed up for Hotmail and tell you your new e-mail address. Click on *Continue at Hotmail*.

12. You are now back at the first screen, except this time you have an account name and a password. Type in your account name, your password, and click *Sign In* as shown in Figure 6-2.

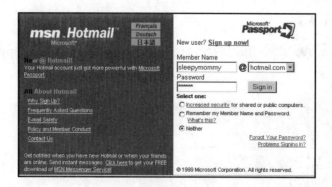

<Figure 6-2> Sign in with your name and password.

The next screen is the reason why Hotmail can afford to give you a free e-mail account—advertisements. In a service called WebCourier, Hotmail allows you to choose the topics for ads that you are willing to receive solicitations for in your e-mail. Choose as many or as few as you like, and click the *Send My WebCourier* button at the bottom of the screen.

Free Web-Based Electronic Mail *(cont.)*

Sending E-mail Using Microsoft Hotmail

You should be looking at the main screen for your e-mail. This screen is called your mailbox. Figure 6-3 shows an example mailbox. If you have said "yes" to any of the previous subscription opportunities, you will already have e-mail. You will want to spend some time here to become familiar with all the ways to get the most out of your e-mail account.

<Figure 6-3> Hotmail mailbox for "sleepymommy"

1. Click on the *Compose* button in your mailbox. Figure 6-4 shows the e-mail form you fill out with the address of the person you are sending the e-mail to, the subject of your e-mail, and the text of your message.

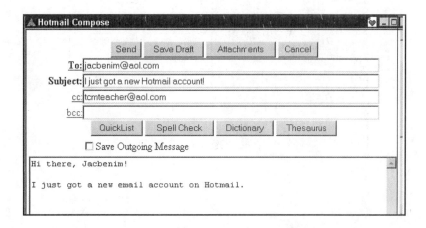

<Figure 6-4> Hotmail compose page example

Free Web-Based Electronic Mail *(cont.)*

2. In the *To:* box, enter the e-mail address of the person you want to send this message to. You may need to click in the box to get move your cursor there so you can type.

3. You should type a few words in the Subject box that reflect the content of your message. It is not necessary to have a subject for your mail to be delivered. However, it usually helps the recipient know what your message will be about.

4. The *cc:* (carbon copy) box is a place for you to enter the e-mail addresses of other people you want to have a copy of this message. The *bcc:* box is used for blind carbon copies. "Blind" means that the recipient will not know who else you sent your message to.

   Note: While "carbon copy" might be considered an outdated term for use with e-mail, this is what Hotmail calls this feature. Some people prefer to think of it as a "courtesy copy."

5. Now click on the large box in the middle of the screen. This is the message box. Type the text of your e-mail message here.

6. Click the *Send* button.

7. After your message has been sent, you will see a Sent Message Confirmation Screen.

8. Click OK.

9. You should be back in your mailbox screen. Take some time to explore the other features of your e-mail service. For additional information, read the online Help.

10. Click *Sign Out* to exit Hotmail.

Technology Take-Off Point

Microsoft Hotmail is only one free full feature Web-based e-mail services available to you. Netscape, which is owned by America Online, also provides a free e-mail service. Access it at the following Web site:

http://webmail.netscape.com

Internet Mailing Lists

Activity

Internet electronic mailing lists are a good way for you to connect with other educators. Mailing lists are exactly what they sound like they are—lists of people who participate in the same e-mail discussion or receive the same e-mailed newsletter. Internet mailing lists are an excellent way to get up-to-date information and provide a way for you to discuss your ideas with other interested participants.

People maintain mailing lists for a variety of reasons. Some are run by businesses that want to advertise their products and services, send press releases, or keep their clients and stockholders informed about changes. Some Web site operators allow you to subscribe to their mailing list so you will be notified whenever changes are made to their Web sites. Some mailing lists are maintained by people who are enthusiasts about specific topics such movie stars, historical figures, or collectibles. Others are maintained by educators who want to share ideas with fellow educators.

Mailing list operators provide information to subscribers about a particular subject. In addition, some list operators also facilitate discussions about the list topics that may occur between the subscribers on the list. Some lists are not facilitated, so an open discussion can result without any rules. Depending on how the mailing list is run, you might feel like you are participating in an organized discussion group or a heated free-for-all debate.

Using mailing lists is not just for businesses or educational forums—many clubs, PTAs, families, neighborhood associations, and churches are starting Internet mailing lists too. You can find lists on a wide variety of subjects.

In this activity, you will learn how to find and subscribe to mailing lists that appeal to you. In addition, you will learn how to unsubscribe in case you ever want your name removed from a mailing list.

Materials

- classroom computer
- Internet Service Provider (ISP)
- e-mail account

Directions

Subscribing to an Internet Mailing List

1. Begin by logging onto your Internet Service Provider (ISP). Start your Internet browser.
2. Go to your favorite search engine. If you do not have one yet, go to Ask Jeeves at the following address:

   http://www.ask.com

3. Type in the question, "Where can I find a list of mailing lists?"

Internet Mailing Lists *(cont.)*

4. Browse the search results to see the quantity and variety of mailing lists that are available. Notice that some of the results of this search are indexes or lists of other mailing lists. There are many good sources of lists. Three that that are easy to search, provide good help features, and a supply a wide variety of lists to choose from are:

http://www.liszt.com

http://www.topica.com

http://www.tile.net

5. Go to the Liszt Web page, which is shown in Figure 7-1.

<Figure 7.1> Liszt home page

6. If you do not see Liszt in your search results, simply type the address (**http://www.liszt.com**) in the Internet address box at the top of your browser.

7. Notice that Liszt has two ways to search for lists. You can type keywords into a search engine or you can click on hyperlinks in a menu. Choose the first method and type "early childhood" as the keywords in the search box. Then click Go.

8. Click on the list name ECENET-L. Notice that you come to a page that allows you to get information about the list. Some people prefer to do this before they subscribe. Other people subscribe if they think a list sounds interesting. Later they unsubscribe if they do not like the list.

<Figure 7-2> Information about subscribing to ECENET-L

9. If this list is interesting to you, then follow the instructions for signing up. In this case, you send your e-mail to **listserv@postoffice.cso.uiuc.edu**. The only words in the e-mail message should be *info ECENET-L*. Then send your e-mail. This will notify the list operator that you are interested in joining the list and that you want more information.

Internet Mailing Lists *(cont.)*

10. The list operator will send you e-mail usually within minutes. The information will include how to subscribe to the list. All you have to do is reply to the list operator's e-mail is to send the following message: *Subscribe ECENET-L.*

11. Now just watch your e-mail for news, information, and discussions. Be ready to write back and participate in your new virtual community.

To Unsubscribe to an Internet Mailing List

When a list no longer suits your needs, dropping your membership is easy. Simply send the list operator an e-mail with the following message: *Unsubscribe ECENET-L.*

Technology Take-Off Point

Give yourself a chance to try several lists over a period of time until you find one that you like. Unless you have a strong desire to teach other teachers, be careful about being drawn into becoming the topic expert on an e-mail list. Be sure you get something out of it for yourself, or move on to try another list.

For most lists, there is one e-mail address for subscribing, unsubscribing, obtaining information, and getting help. There is a different e-mail address for participating in topic discussions. Everything you mail to the discussion address goes to everyone on the list. Normally all the administrative and discussion messages are automatically managed by computer and are not reviewed or moderated by people. Keep these two addresses separate. Discussion group members would prefer not to read mail about subscribing and unsubscribing to the list.

Saving Images and Pictures to Disk

Activity

The Internet offers vast resources of pictures and images that you can easily download and save on your computer for use in your classroom. Learning this simple skill will enable you to use the graphic images and photographs that are available on the Internet.

Be sure to use antivirus software (page 14) when accessing and downloading information, graphics, and photographs from the Internet.

Materials

- classroom computer
- Internet Service Provider (ISP)
- Windows 95 or better or MAC operating system
- hard drive space or floppy disks
- antivirus software (page 14)

Directions

1. Log onto the Internet and find a picture you like. Remember that copyright laws exist on the Internet, but most sites allow educational use of materials. Read the site carefully, and contact the Web master if you are not sure about using a picture on a site.
2. For a PC, point to the image and right-click. You will see a floating menu. For a MAC, click and hold. A floating menu will appear.
3. For a PC, click Save Picture As. The Save As dialog box appears, allowing you to decide where you want to save the image. Name the image in the File name textbox and click Save. For a MAC, click Save this image as… You will see the Save As dialog box, allowing you to save the image. Select Save to Desktop and the image will be saved, making it available as a file icon located on your desktop.

Technology Take-Off Point

The most basic antivirus software does not cost very much and provides important protection for your computer. Ask your local software dealer to give you information about the different kinds of antivirus software that are available.